# KISSING A FROG

## FOUR STEPS TO FINDING COMFORT OUTSIDE YOUR COMFORT ZONE

### SHARLENE HAWKES

**SHADOW MOUNTAIN**

*Excerpt from* Seabiscuit *by Laura Hillenbrand, copyright © 2001 by Laura Hillenbrand. Used by permission of Random House, Inc. and HarperCollins Publishers Ltd.*

Visit us at www.shadowmountain.com

**Library of Congress Cataloging-in-Publication Data**

Hawkes, Sharlene Wells, 1964–
   Kissing a frog : four steps to finding comfort outside your comfort zone / Sharlene Hawkes.
     p.    cm.
    ISBN 1-57008-875-6
    1. Self-actualization (Psychology)   I. Title.

BF637.S4 H378 2002
158.1—dc21                             2002010863

Printed in the United States of America       72076-300178
Publishers Printing, Salt Lake City, UT

10  9  8  7  6  5  4  3  2

*To Bob,*

*for your sustaining love and patience*

# CONTENTS

## STEP 3: WORK WITH THE TOOLS THAT WILL HELP YOU DO THE HARD THINGS

## STEP 4: UNDERSTAND THE PRACTICAL POINTS OF LEAVING YOUR COMFORT ZONE

Introduction

# RECOGNIZING WHAT LIES OUTSIDE YOUR COMFORT ZONE

As a schoolgirl I never imagined I would someday be paid to speak to large audiences. Why not? Standing in front of people to speak, perform, or even just stand there scared me to death. I remember the first time I gathered enough courage to run for office. I was in the sixth grade and terrified. When the time came to deliver my campaign speech, a frightening lump kept rising in my throat, interfering with my ability to breathe and the important words I had to say.

I hated being in a position where everyone was looking only at me. I was certain they could see how nervous I was. And then, when I not only lost the election but also picked up the fewest votes of any of the candidates, getting up in front of another group of people ever again seemed absolutely impossible. *Why would I want to put myself through that pain again?* Even now, I can vividly remember what it was like to be so scared I could hardly speak. And yet, years later I am in a profession that requires constant scrutiny by large audiences and almost-daily "performances" of some sort or another. How did *that* happen?

How I became Miss America is an even bigger mystery to me. Growing up, I was a honest-to-goodness tomboy. I didn't like dolls, frilly things, dresses (*still* don't), or girls (they were always crying about something). I did like soccer balls, footballs, and softballs. And though I was never an outstanding athlete, I participated in any team that would let me join. Those who knew me back then are still in shock that I left my comfort zone on the playing field and sports court and figured out how to walk in a pair of high heels.

What they don't know is that I am an expert on comfort zones; my entire life has been built around a consistent pattern of leaving them. Becoming Miss America and then working as a full-time and now free-lance sports broadcaster for seventeen years were both roles outside my boundaries of comfort. The minute I arrived in Atlantic City in 1984 for the Miss America pageant, I felt out of place—like an outsider looking in, or someone hoping to crash a party. I felt like a high school freshman all over again. Everyone else there seemed to know what to do and what to wear. I felt outclassed and light-years out of my comfort zone. I wanted so much to go find a racquetball court.

The only reason I had made it to Atlantic City was very simple. My fear of being a coward—of having no courage at all—was much greater than my fear of failure. If I had backed down from an opportunity for a cash scholarship in the Miss America program just because I might have failed, then I would have considered myself a coward.

And then there was the moment I arrived at ESPN headquarters in Bristol, Connecticut, as a twenty-three-year-old network novice. I kept wondering how long it would take them to discover I was a phony. As much as I loved sports, I didn't know every statistic in the book. I was there because I loved covering competition—*any* kind of competition. I loved talking to players, finding out how they became champions, and learning how they coped with loss. But the TV camera itself was an intensely intimidating object. Even though I knew how to make myself look comfortable and natural on screen, I was a nervous wreck before the little red light went on. Regardless of these fears, I took the opportunity to work in TV sports because, once again, my distaste for cowardice was greater than my fear of failure. I couldn't imagine turning down a job offer—especially such an amazing one—just because I might have made a fool of myself.

## FROM STAGE FRIGHT TO STAGE PRESENCE

It is widely believed that most people in the entertainment/television/speaking industry have loved doing what they do ever since they were precocious youngsters, falling all over themselves just for a chance to grab the spotlight. Not me. As a young girl I dreamed of being a veterinarian, an architect, or maybe even an international business whiz. I really *hated* being in the spotlight. I dreaded the possibility that my nerves would take over completely and leave me feeling like a helpless mess of wet noodles. I agonized over the noose that I knew would inevitably constrict my throat just before I had to give an oral report in class. I feared the complete loss of support from my useless knees and the ensuing embarrassment that would inevitably result from my fall to the floor. The stage, in all its forms, was not my home. It was somewhere outside of my comfort zone in "a galaxy far, far away."

So what happened? How did I go from there . . . to

here? From stage fright to stage presence? Well, it all has to do with one decision I made early on, a decision that has affected every choice I have made since then. I decided to accept *challenge*. I wanted to be courageous, not cowardly. This forced me to learn the nature of my comfort zone and discover the great role that *challenge* plays in creating a meaningful, enriching life.

## A REALISTIC REACH

Since the day I made the decision to accept *challenge,* my comfort zone has become both my partner and my primary antagonist. I have learned that all worthy competitors must explore these two elements of their comfort zones to become champions. Within my comfort zone I find the crucial support that holds me up and pushes me to do more, much the way a winning coach pushes his star athlete. Waiting just outside the boundaries of my comfort zone is my antagonist, the challenge of the unknown—the "what ifs" and "why nots" that are the opponents. To face them brings the possibility of success. To default brings the confirmation of failure.

While there are many things that still appear to rest outside of my comfort zone, I have made that zone large enough that nothing I want to do feels so completely out of reach that I cannot *realistically* hope to achieve it. Being realistic is important because a successful life demands that we set priorities and abide by the rules that accompany those priorities; then we can allow our dreams to fly unfettered.

My priority, for example, is my family. Therefore, I let myself dream of all the things I can do and want to do that will allow me to place my family above all other commitments and responsibilities. Some people may believe that my decision is unwise and doesn't allow me to succeed personally. What they don't realize is that I have set my priorities with the knowledge that *my own* real happiness comes from success in my home and in my relationships. If I forsake that priority to pursue a different dream, I'm essentially shooting myself in the foot. So I don't dream of being an astronaut or an Olympian. Both would take training that would require me to personally sacrifice my priorities. And besides, I'm really not smart enough to be an astronaut or fast enough to be an Olympian. If I were, my priorities would be arranged differently for a while. Instead, I focus on dreams that will work with my priorities, not against them. This enables a *realistic* reach outside of my comfort zone.

## DEFINING YOUR ZONE

Everyone has a comfort zone. Even you. And how do I know that you have a comfort zone?

I grew up in South America and have traveled the world over (including all fifty states). Meeting and speaking with thousands of people of all backgrounds and inclinations has taught me that there isn't anyone who doesn't have some type of comfort zone, be it large or small. Brain surgeons and garbage collectors. Hair stylists and CEOs. Professional ball players and schoolteachers. They all have comfort zones. A business executive who is suddenly left alone at home for a few hours to care for a three year old and a crying baby with messy diapers may well be challenging the borders of his comfort zone. So is the student who finds herself in a harder class than she expected. Or the doctor who clams up when it is his turn to give an oral presentation. And what about the single mother who has no marketable skills to brag about but must find a job? Or the salesman who can't swing a golf club to get a soccer ball off the tee but has a dozen clients who love to golf.

We are all better at some things than at others. And most of us tend to construct our own comfort zones around those things in which we excel. After all, stepping outside the boundaries of our comfort zones is about as appealing as kissing a frog.

Kissing a frog—let alone flirting with it a little at first—is not most people's idea of a romantic evening. In fact, it's quite disgusting. If you remember the fairy tale, however, you know that the end results of that storied kiss from a lovely princess to a wart-covered toad far exceeded the princess's imagination. She did something *hard,* something she really didn't want to do but knew she should . . . and she was rewarded for her efforts. She got herself a prince. Her fairy-tale life is worth the effort it took to kiss that frog—and now that princess is probably a lot more likely to hang around with things that look a bit slimy on the outside.

Like our famous princess, I have discovered that the boundaries of our comfort zones are not immovable. We *can* do the hard things. In reality, the borders that once seemed so straight and concrete are quite fluid, which means they can always be changed—and we can always learn to like the frogs we have to kiss.

I like to think of my comfort zone as a pond. A pond's unique ecosystem is constantly challenged. Regular exposure to wind, rain, and other environmental elements causes its shorelines to expand and contract continually. Sometimes a pond may be so full of water it floods into the surrounding swamp, creating streamlets that connect it from one pond to another. At other times it can be rather dry, causing the water at the edges to become shallow.

A pond, just like a comfort zone, is full of life. Frogs, toads, insects, and any number of other creatures enjoy the water and plant life the pond provides. When flooding occurs, new life may venture into the pond; and sometimes this new life can stir up the waters quite a bit. This book is all about that new life and reaching out to embrace it as you broaden your own comfort zone. So come along; let's go see about kissing that frog. You never know when it might magically turn into a prince!

*Step 1*

# APPRECIATE THE DYNAMIC NATURE OF YOUR COMFORT ZONE

Letting Fresh Water into
a Dead, Stagnant Pond

*Determining Why, Exactly,
You Would Want to Kiss a
Frog in the First Place*

Chapter 1

# USING PERSONAL CHALLENGES TO CREATE A MEANINGFUL LIFE

What does a comfort zone look like, and why is it important to challenge its borders on occasion?

A comfort zone is the circle we draw around all those things with which we are perfectly comfortable. Within that circle is a pond, so to speak, that is full of life and the dynamic circumstances that sometimes lead us to venture near the borders of the zone and even outside it.

Within the zone are at least two areas that determine how we behave and react to the elements surrounding us. The first area is labeled *me and others*. It is all about our interaction with those around us.

The second area is labeled *me and me*. It has to do with the only thing each of us can control—ourselves. It includes how we choose to deal with the things that happen to us, how we challenge ourselves, and the types of decisions we make.

Most of us tend to swim between these two areas of the pond on a regular basis. This is because they are full of the things we like to do and are good at doing—the things that are easy. The first area includes such activities as getting together with a bunch of close friends for an Independence Day barbecue. The second area might include lying in a hammock reading your favorite book or working in your garage on a project that's meaningful to you and showcases one of your talents.

Outside the pond, in the swampy areas surrounding it, are all those things we don't like to do. And why don't we like them? Well, as my husband always says, "You only hate things you don't understand." Anything we are not good at will probably fall into the category of things we don't like to do. These may include struggles such as offering an apology, maintaining an exercise routine, accompanying a spouse to a social event, volunteering in a child's classroom, and so on.

Finally, all those things that we *can* do but *don't like* to do rest just on the edge of the pond; they really could go either way. Sometimes, the more we do something we dislike, the easier it becomes. And eventually it will fall into the pond. On the other hand, the task may become harder and more complicated the more we do it. In this case, it heads into the swamp and sometimes even aims upward for outer space. For example, let's say you are a good swimmer and decide to start learning the butterfly stroke. You discover, however, that it is harder and more frustrating than you thought it would be. Pretty soon you are waterlogged and have no desire to see another swimming pool for the rest of the summer. For a while, at least, swimming is out of your comfort zone.

## ARE YOU A WALLFLOWER?

Most people tend to feel that everything outside of their comfort zones should be labeled "Danger: Experimental

Area" or "Construction in Progress—Must Have Your Hard Hat on Because You Are Bound to Encounter Hard Knocks." And when it comes to something such as how we feel about ourselves, experimenting with the borders of our comfort zones is not usually a chance we want to take, especially if anyone is watching. For that very reason, my husband hates to dance. He doesn't want to get out on the dance floor where everyone can see him "experiment." And he doesn't like to draw attention to himself in the first place, so he'd rather be a wallflower than risk being noticed. I feel the same way about my dancing, but sometimes the music is just too irresistible and I find myself tapping my feet. I can usually get away with just a few snickers from the audience if I grab my four-year-old son to dance with.

I would guess that at least 50 percent of us sit on the sidelines and watch as the other 50 percent venture out to the dance floor and get into the beat. On the dance floor, both my husband and I are usually part of the first 50 percent—the wallflowers. But a wallflower at a dance is not a wallflower everywhere. We all have our areas of expertise and our areas of inability or inexperience. The problem is that many people become wallflowers in too many areas of their lives because they have given things a try and felt foolish in the end. And because no one likes to appear foolish, many decide that it is better to simply blend in. *If I don't do anything different, I won't ever look foolish,* they reason. *No one will laugh at me or tease me.*

Why are we so concerned about what our peers think of what we are doing, wearing, or saying? One of my favorite quotes is by Earl Nightingale. He said, "You wouldn't worry so much about what other people thought of you if you only realized how little they did." Exactly. Most people are too worried about *themselves* to really care about what *you* are doing! And for those who *can* put on blinders and remain oblivious to the possible embarrassment of total failure, it is usually cheers—and not jeers—that await them.

## CROSSING THE FINISH LINE

I began working for ESPN in 1987, when I was just twenty-three years old. For the next seven years I remained on contract until my children came along. At that time, I pulled back to free-lance status and have continued covering exciting events on a limited basis. One of my favorite things about working for ESPN is the chance that I have had to witness firsthand how athletes deal with very public failures—often turning them into moments of great inspiration for the rest of us.

A few years ago, for example, I was on assignment, covering the National High School Track and Field Championships. My job was to grab the winners for a brief post-event television interview. As you might imagine, there was quite a collection of young talent at this national meet. The final day of the event was long, hot, and muggy, and by late afternoon I was more than anxious to wrap things up. By this time the field events were over and the athletes had cleared out of the infield. The spectators in the stands had dwindled down to about five hundred, and you could tell they were moving around, gathering their things, and getting ready to leave after the last race. One of the final events was the boys' two-mile run. The gun went off, but I barely noticed as I alternately collected my papers, watched the race, and took a few notes. It wasn't one of those races that required constant attention . . . or so I thought.

About midway through the race, when I finally began to pay attention, I could see that one runner was beginning to leave the pack behind. So I began to busily write down some questions for him. Right about then, I gradually became aware of an unusual silence in the stadium, so I looked over to the stands to see everyone intently watching the track. I quickly followed the audience's gaze as the runners passed by, but I didn't see anything out of the ordinary—just one boy way out in front. Noticing my slight confusion, my producer leaned over and whispered as he pointed to the boy, "He's about to be lapped." The boy who I had assumed was in the lead was actually last, and the rest of the pack was about to lap him. *Oh no, I thought, don't let them lap you—not in front of all these people, and especially our ESPN cameras.*

But the inevitable did happen. About twenty other runners lapped the boy. And again, this was just halfway through the race. A few minutes later as the runners neared the finish line, it looked like the last runner was about to be lapped again. Mercifully, the winner crossed the finish line, arms in the air, just before reaching the boy. There were cheers for the winner, I quickly ran over to him with our camera, and we were all focused on the victor now. But as we wrapped up, I again noticed that things had quieted down. I looked once again to the track.

I guess I had wrongly assumed that this boy, with nearly two laps left to finish the race, would quietly run off the track and escape to some hiding place. But he didn't. He kept plodding along. And on his final, long, solo lap around the track, the spectators, athletes, and coaches who had been prepared to leave were now on their feet, cheering the runner home. As he crossed the finish line, the crowd went wild. You would have thought he had just won the gold instead of finishing dead last.

Now, I don't know if he was injured or sick or just plain out-classed, but the last runner left a greater impression on me that day than any of the winners did. Why did we stand for him and applaud his valiant, spine-tingling efforts? It was because he had just turned a very humiliating experience into a heroic one. We admired him. We wanted to be like him. We wanted his courage so that we could boldly and bravely leave our own comfort zones.

That young man challenged the walls of his comfort zone and broke through. I noticed when he crossed the finish line that the look on his face was completely different from the one he had shown when he was lapped. He never would have known that feeling of triumph and recognition had he quit and remained where he was comfortable. His comfort zone grew immensely that day because he became aware of his capabilities to overcome great obstacles.

If that last runner had imagined carrying out such a scenario before the race began, it likely would have fallen outside of his zone. But once he was faced with this hard challenge and decided to tackle it head on, his comfort zone grew to encompass the difficult experience. He had proven to himself that he was no quitter. Just like the ever-expanding universe, our comfort zones can grow—there will always be space beyond the borders. It is that unknown space that worries us and holds us back. In that space are the unknown ramifications of an action taken and the unknown results of putting our trust in someone else. But it is also in the unknown space where we discover talents, personal satisfaction, and hope for the future.

Chapter 2

# FINDING THE RIGHT TIME TO LEAVE YOUR COMFORT ZONE

Knowing when to pucker up and leave your comfort zone is difficult, especially when self-doubts can so easily creep into your mind. Self-doubt inevitably leads to many questions: Do I have what it takes to be successful? What makes me think I can do this? How am I different from others who have tried the same thing? How do I know which chances to take and which to pass up? How do I discover my talents? Here is some practical advice:

First, gather all the information possible on the decision you're about to make, no matter how trivial it may seem. Do research, interview trusted individuals, and write down all the reasons why you should and why you shouldn't move forward with the decision to step outside your comfort zone.

Second, ask yourself, "What is my gut feeling? What is my conscience telling me to do?" In the long run (if not the short), the "right thing to do" will always be the best choice.

Third, remember that sometimes the choice to leave

your comfort zone may be neither right nor wrong. It may simply be a choice of whether or not you want to challenge yourself to do something really hard. So then you can ask, "Will choosing to step outside my comfort zone make me a better person? A better spouse? A better employee? A better friend? A better parent? A better sibling?" If the answer is no, then what's the point?

## THE HARD THINGS

Most of us shun the thought of stepping outside of our comfort zones because it can often mean doing the hard things. On a flight not too long ago I sat next to a man who needed some conversation. He began by giving me his life story. He was divorced and on the road a lot so he didn't get to see his four-year-old daughter very often. As a result, he was considering a new job.

After listening for a while, I began asking him some questions about what he *really* wanted to do with his life and why he hadn't yet made the final decision to get a new job. He started listing all sorts of excuses—the "Oh, woe is me!" kind of excuses. Because I'm not really the sympathetic type when it comes to excuses, I pushed him further to look at the real reasons behind his inaction.

After a few minutes of this he said, "You remind me of my ex-wife!" I assumed that was *not* a compliment but thanked him anyway. I told him she was probably better for him than he realized. He laughed and agreed.

The more we chatted, the simpler his "excuses" became until he finally hit it on the head. It was just too hard. It was too hard to commit to change—to become better. He kept repeating, "Why does it matter anyway? Why can't I just stay the same?" I think I finally convinced him that nothing stays the same. At any point in time, each of us is becoming either better or worse. I asked him if he was deliriously happy and satisfied with his life. After he acknowledged that he wasn't, I looked at him directly and said, "Then that's why it matters." One of the reasons happy people are happy is because they are willing to try new things and challenge themselves. Their lives are not stagnant.

## RUGGED INDIVIDUALISM

Just as early American frontiersmen had the guts to venture into new and unknown territory in the West and tame its wild lands, all of us probably need to be more daring as we discover our talents. Do you remember reading about "rugged individualism" in your history books? Rugged individualism—the courage to venture out on one's own into new territory—is an all-American term coined in the frontier days of our nation's infancy.

In my family, we're very familiar with "rugged individualism." My ancestors on both my mother's and father's sides were pioneers, trekking west in covered wagons and handcarts, leaving the comforts of established civilization for the unknown, and often fearsome, frontier. My great-great-grandfather Edward Bunker was the kind of rugged individualist that legends are made of. Grandpa Bunker was the leader of the third group of pioneers that headed for the Great Salt Lake Valley (it was actually his *fifth* trip across the continent). While they were crossing the plains in Wyoming, a large group of Indians appeared on the bluff ready for war. Their faces were covered with war paint and they carried spears, bows, and arrows. Grandpa Bunker was at the rear of the train when the Indians were first spotted. By the time he reached the head of the wagon train, the people had completely panicked. Women were crying, and the men were shouting, "We'll all be killed! Let's pray, *let's pray!*" When Grandfather Bunker heard these cries, he yelled, "Pray? Hell! I'm up to date on *my* prayers! Circle the wagons, and get ready to fight!" When they saw the wagons circling, the Indians thought twice about their plans and simply left.

A rugged individualist seizes the moment even when there is fear or self-doubt. Those pioneers weren't fearless, but they had something they valued more than fear—they had beautiful visions of what could be if they just showed a little bit of courage. Their horizons were *limitless*.

As a reporter with ESPN, I was sent to interview a young man in Texas who had just broken the state high school rushing record. This was no small feat, even in a state accustomed to producing great talent. I was anxious to meet the athlete with a brilliant future ahead of him. I soon discovered, however, that Robert Strait was not the pampered athlete that so many of the others I interviewed were. He lived in a small house in a small town, where he and his single mother got by on welfare. At times, such circumstances foster hopelessness, self-pity, or even a "the world owes me something" attitude. I found nothing of the kind in Robert. In fact, he said something that has stuck with me more than any of the words spoken to me by a professional or Olympic athlete. When I asked Robert if he felt he had limits, his face registered surprise as though it had never occurred to him. He then responded, "Limits? Nah, I have no limits. If I can run 100 yards, then why not 200? If I can run 200, then why not 300? I go as far as I can see and when I get there, I can see farther." For Robert, poverty and circumstance were a state of mind. So was becoming a champion.

Do you have limits? What is holding you back? Maybe

it's telling yourself, "I can never lose this weight," or, "I can't start my own business—I'm not good at sales and public relations." Perhaps the thoughts, "I could never run for office . . . who would vote for me?" or, "I can't change jobs; no one else would hire me" have entered your mind. Or even, "I'm just a housewife, who would listen to me?" For most of us, the one thing that holds us back is fear. And that's why, many times, we begin to complain and make excuses. After all, most of us feel that if there is a good enough reason not to do something challenging, then we won't even have to try. Our fears can stay at arm's length, with our excuses as the buffer zone.

But wouldn't you like to be known as a rugged individualist—someone who forges into unknown territory, determines his own destiny, sets his own course, and heads toward new personal frontiers? Or are you more content to just follow the manual, carrying on with standard procedure and sticking to what everyone else is doing? Every now and then it's okay to be a little out of control in an adventurous sort of way. Once, as my second oldest daughter—then five years old—skied past me at breakneck speed, I yelled, "Nicole, ski in control!" She shouted back as I sped to catch up with her, "But I don't want to be in control!" Now, that's a scary way to look at things if you're doing something physically dangerous, but have you ever just let your mind fly out of control, thinking of all you could possibly do to make your world, and your life, better?

## ONE LEAGUE AT A TIME

Have you ever been on a boat at sea and gazed at the endless ocean? If you have, then you probably felt small at that moment and perhaps a bit intimidated by the sheer enormity of the vast horizon. You might have even wondered, "How will we ever cross this ocean?" Well, the answer is simple. The ocean is crossed one league at a time.

Likewise, success is all about dreaming big but starting small—taking small chances and building on them. In fact, true greatness lies in the small decisions you make along the way.

Why is it important to start making small attempts to stick out your neck and discover what you're made of? It is important because if you don't know who you are, what you stand for, what you're made of, and what you're good at, then chances are that someone else will decide for you! Someone else will be the leader, and you will just be the follower. That's perfectly fine if you are working on a project with a group of people and someone else is the chief. But it doesn't work in everyday life. You are the only one in charge of discovering what makes you YOU! Knowing yourself and why you are unique will help you to build on your individuality and use it toward your own success.

## FINDING A HOOK

For reporters, the first step in defining any story is finding "the hook." A reporter must ask, What makes this story different? Why am I telling this story? If there is no hook—or nothing to individualize the story—then it is not aired.

So there you have it. Find your hook. Everyone has one, and it's the most likely place to find success. But finding that hook can be risky, tricky, and even scary because it means you have to search, dig, and undergo a process of trials and errors. Yuck! Wouldn't you much rather grab a book and go sit in a hammock on a beach in the Caribbean for a while? I think most of us would! So, if this "experimental" process sounds downright torturous, try looking at it from another angle.

Look at it as an adventure—a treasure hunt to find all the things you *can* do!

But remember, this adventure doesn't necessarily have a destination; rather, it's a continual challenge of your comfort zone's boundaries. After someone wins the Super Bowl or becomes a CEO or funds his retirement, should the adventure of pushing his or her comfort zone outward end?

Think about what happens to a stagnant pond that receives no fresh water to replenish it. No matter how beautiful the pond's setting, things start to stink when fresh water is unavailable and the winds are too calm to stir up any ripples or waves.

When championship basketball coach Rick Pitino decided to leave the University of Kentucky (where he was in a comfortable position, having led the team to a national championship in 1996) to take the head position at the Boston Celtics, he made an interesting comment. When asked why he would move out of such a desirable situation, where he was popular and highly paid, he said his main reason for leaving was simply that he was too young to be comfortable. He was forty-five years old at the time and was far from ready to settle for the easy life.

I suppose until we're old enough to start getting social security checks, we just might all be too young to be comfortable. "Being comfortable" can, after all, mean being *resigned*. And accepting resignation is often a sign of defeat. Naturally, "being comfortable" can also mean that you are comfortable! And there is nothing wrong with being comfortable, unless it has something to do with resignation or defeat. That's when you should take a good hard look at why you're sitting in the recliner. Sometimes you do need to relax and go easy on yourself. But other times you have to give yourself a kick.

## GOING IN CIRCLES

When my daughter Sarah was three years old, she loved to hang around our exercise room and watch me work out. One morning my husband, Bob, and I were both lifting weights in our basement while she went about her usual investigation of the exercise equipment we have collected. Suddenly, she stopped her busywork to watch the two of us as we began lifting. With a growing expression of concern, she walked right over to us and asked, "Mom and Dad? Why are you being so mean to yourselves?" With our laughter taking the strength right out of us, we could see her point of view! We did look like we were doing something terribly mean to ourselves—the sweat pouring down our faces, the scary grimaces. For a moment I thought, *Yeah, what are we doing to ourselves! Really, why should I be "mean" to myself? What am I hoping to accomplish?*

The reason for lifting weights is obvious—to stay fit and build muscle tone, to challenge the human body's ability to endure. But why should you challenge yourself in other areas?

Well, one reason is trivial but is nevertheless an important aspect of mental health.

You need variety in your life. If all you do is go in circles, you eventually begin to spiral downward.

Let me illustrate.

Several years ago I was in Reno, Nevada, hosting a special on the World Gliding Championships. I was impressed by the simple beauty of the gliders. These delicate flying machines have no engine—just a fuselage with very long, skinny wings. They don't appear to be very durable machines. To take flight, the gliders are towed behind an airplane until they reach an altitude high enough to be released, at which time the pilot finds the best air currents to ride as long as possible. I had never ridden in one of these gliders, so when the producer suggested that I climb in the backseat of a two-seater and let the world champion pilot me on a quiet ride, I jumped at the chance.

My camera crew set up two different cameras to record my adventure. I buckled up and locked the bubble canopy into place. Then came our takeoff. It was a very hot day, but it got even hotter when I realized there was no air conditioner in this thing—just a small hole in the canopy to let in some air. To make matters worse, I had no shade in which to hide from the sun beating down through the bubble that seemed to be acting as a kind of prism for the sun's rays. I was getting pretty warm, to say the least.

Finally the airplane released us, and we were on our own. The pilot began to explain to me that we would ride the same current that eagles and hawks soar on as they search for food. Gradually it began to dawn on me that he was talking about *circles*. We would be going around in circles for the next half hour!

Now, think about the last time you were at the amusement park on a ride that just went in circles. For half an hour we went in circles, spiraling lower and lower until we were close enough to the ground to land at the private airport. I was feeling green by this time and was more than happy to land. After landing, my producer came running over and said he would like me to go up again because they wanted to put a tiny camera on the end of the wing to give viewers the perspective of looking back at the pilot and me. I wanted to be a good sport so I said sure. I could do it one more time.

So up we went again. Because I knew the cameras were now watching my every move, I tried to be cheerful about the whole thing. By the time we landed, everything was spinning around me. But at least I was on the ground and I could begin recuperating. Again, the producer ran over with another great idea. "I'd like you to go up one last time, and this time we'll tape a little camera to the inside of the cockpit looking right at you. Then we'll get great reaction shots to edit in!" I tried hard to be as excited as he was with this great new idea. Before the canopy was closed again, my producer gave me a remote for the camera. He was running low on battery so he told me to not turn it on until we were released from the airplane tow.

I don't remember much of the third flight up, just that I didn't want to be there. I was done being adventurous. I just wanted terra firma. But I was there, so when we began gliding on our own, I turned on the camera. You wouldn't believe how excited I looked—I was pointing at this and that, asking the pilot questions, smiling. But then I knew something was really wrong. I felt sick—to my stomach. I had visions of something embarrassing happening on camera and then being played over and over on all the national bloopers shows. No way. Not me. I turned off the camera, grabbed for an airsick bag, used the airsick bag, and cleaned myself up. Then I turned the camera back on with a big smile on my face. No one even noticed. They thought it was a glitch on the tape.

I knew it wasn't a glitch. I also knew that I would never let myself go in circles again. Going in circles accomplishes only one thing: regurgitation. That may not *literally* happen when you can't break out of a routine and find new challenges (although it's certainly a possibility). In order to lead a full life, however, you must be willing to follow different patterns. Look for new horizons now and then.

## THE POWER OF *CHALLENGE*

In addition to the need for variety, you should consider another, more profound, reason to accept and seek out change. In 1986, as a cub sports reporter with KSL-TV in Salt Lake City, I was assigned to cover a wheelchair racing clinic featuring one of the world's most outstanding wheelchair athletes. His name was Jim Knaub, and he was a world record holder several times over in the ever-growing competitive and grueling sport of wheelchair racing. In fact, he holds the record for winning the Boston Marathon *five* times in his division! His fascinating demonstration/lecture was punctuated with stories of triumph . . . and disaster. He even showed the latest in racing equipment—lightweight, high-tech, low-profile and completely aerodynamic racing chairs.

Following his presentation, Jim graciously gave me some time for an interview. My first question was basic but launched him into a comprehensive view of his philosophy of life. "So, how did you get started in the sport?" I asked. Jim then explained that all of his life he had wanted to compete in the Olympics and had in fact become one of the best pole-vaulters in the country. With his refined skills, he was expected to compete in the 1984 Los Angeles Olympics. Just months before the Summer Olympics, however, a terrible accident occurred. Jim was on his motorcycle, idling at a stoplight, when an elderly gentleman drove up in back of him and accidentally pressed the gas pedal instead of stepping on the brakes. Jim was paralyzed from the waist down as a result.

He described for me the agonizing weeks and months that followed—the blame, the anger, the self-pity, the sorrow surrounding broken dreams, not to mention the pain. Then, roughly two months following the accident, as Jim lay in a rehabilitation center, he turned the corner of despair.

The TV in Jim's room was on and the Boston Marathon drew his attention. It was raining hard in Boston, and runners were drenched as they slogged through the streets. Suddenly, the camera focused on a lone wheelchair racer, struggling uphill against the sheets of rain. The network stayed with him for a while, and Jim watched—mesmerized. He said to himself, "I can still challenge myself. I *want* to do that. Give me something difficult! It doesn't matter what I think my limits are, I can still be challenged." The right time had come for him to make his move.

Until he saw that broadcast, Jim hadn't realized how vital it is to both our mental and physical health to be continually challenged. Jim realized that his need to be challenged could serve as a catalyst for developing healthy self-esteem and self-respect. Jim did take up the sport; he dedicated himself to excellence along an altogether different path and continues to make a significant contribution in raising the level of respect that is given to athletes with disabilities.

Challenge feeds the soul just as fresh water feeds a pond. It not only prevents foul-smelling stagnation but it can also create a larger and larger pond. Even if fresh water is accumulated one little drop at a time, the new life in that pond will notice the difference; and one drop—like one ounce of courage—will quickly begin to expand the boundaries of your comfort zone.

Chapter 3

# UNDERSTANDING
# THE NATURE
# OF COURAGE

Once you realize the time is right to make your move, take a close look at the dimensions of your comfort zone. Keep in mind that doing so requires you to study the nature of courage. Why? Because it is courage, or the lack thereof, that either takes you out of or keeps you inside your comfort zone. But how much courage do you need to actually kiss a frog?

Two prevalent myths exist when it comes to courage. The first: If you have courage, you must not have fear. That might sound right when you hear it, but read it again and really think about it. Of course you can have both courage and fear at the same time! When someone first attempts skydiving, do you think he's unafraid? No way! He just closes his eyes, sucks it up, and jumps anyway.

One summer my husband, four children, and I were invited by a friend to go waterskiing on a nearby lake. It was an enjoyable afternoon until unexpected storm clouds darkened the sky, bringing with them lightning and high winds. The waves swelled higher and higher as the rain pelted down on us.

Soon, the waves began to crash onto the boat. To protect the children, we covered the bow of the ski boat with the customized tarp and had the kids move under there. The boat continued to take on water and moved as if on a roller coaster. My husband and I could not help *feeling* fearful. Because we are parents, however, and it does no good to let our children know when we are scared, we managed to downplay the severity of our situation. We joked with the kids, asked them if they liked the fun ride, reminded them of the water rides they like so much, and reassured them that we were almost done. Our three year old very calmly said that she didn't like this ride and didn't want to go again, thank you very much. Yes we were fearful, but none of the children remembers that traumatic time because we let our courage override our fear.

The second myth goes something like this: in order to have courage, you must have *a lot* of courage. But if that were true, imagine all of the unfinished adventures and inventions you'd be reading about in the papers. When it comes to courage, all you really need is one drop—just enough to take one tiny step outside your comfort zone. And then something remarkable happens. Your comfort zone grows! The more you step outside of its original boundaries, the more it grows. And likewise, the more you stay within it, the smaller it gets. Just one drop of courage moves you beyond the boundary, and that's really the scariest part. Once you get moving, momentum kicks in.

## THE SURVIVAL INSTINCT

Sadly, some people tell me, "But I don't have any courage!" And my answer to them is always, "Oh, yes you do!" Everyone was born with courage. You might call it a "survival instinct," but it's the same thing.

A few years ago my husband and I became instant friends with a remarkable man—someone America called a hero. Captain Scott O'Grady was shot down over Bosnia on June 2, 1995, and for six days waited for rescue as he eluded capture by the enemy. When he was finally rescued by equally extraordinary and courageous Marines, he was brought home amidst all the fanfare usually showered on returning heroes. But in his book *Return with Honor* (New York: Doubleday, 1995), Scott viewed himself differently: "For the record, I don't consider myself a hero. As I see it, I was a guy in the wrong place at the wrong time. In seventy thousand Deny Flight sorties over Bosnia, only two pilots had been shot down through June 1995; I happened to win that dubious lottery. Before the missile rudely interrupted me, I was simply serving my country, doing my job. Once the *fait* was *accompli,* I used my training to make the best of a grim situation. . . . As I huddled in those woods, I didn't feel like Captain Scott O'Grady, fighter pilot. I was just a scared guy named Scott, getting by on his wits, discovering more about himself each day. I gained a new sense of self-worth, and it had nothing to do with any medals or decorations" (199, 203).

Every now and then we tease Captain O'Grady about the "grilled bugs" we might have for dinner, or about being "wimpy" because of the layers *and layers* of clothing he wears during cold weather, but that's only because we know he's already passed the test of courage. He's got nothing to prove—ever. He'll chuckle when we talk about his thermal clothing and say something like, "I'm *never* going to be that cold again! Not if I can help it!"

## REAL COURAGE RUNS DEEP

Now, it is important to remember that courage isn't the same as "bravado"—a "daredevil" doesn't truly possess the type of courage that changes lives. In fact, a daredevil may have the capacity to *ruin* lives. Last year, just down the street from my home, a teenager in his sports car decided he wanted to show how "brave" he was by challenging a motorcyclist to a race down the frontage road. To make it really "courageous," they raced late at night without head-lights. As they tore down the road, a young woman from my neighborhood unsuspectingly pulled out onto the road—immediately in front of the black sports car. She was killed instantly. Her mother lived next to the parents of this "daredevil."

What that teenage boy possessed doesn't even resemble real courage. Real courage runs deep and belongs to anyone who is willing to get up and keep moving. Cavett Robert, the founder of the National Speakers Association to which I belong, said, "It may be true that life is a grind-stone, but it is equally true that whether it grinds us or polishes us is determined alone by the substance of which we are made. . . . That which has proved to be a stumbling block to one individual is a stepping-stone to a more coura-geous soul."

## ACTING ON YOUR COURAGE

I remember being much younger and wishing that I had the courage I saw in others. It seemed so easy for others to get up in front of people and speak or perform. They never looked as scared as I felt. Just standing in front of an audience was enough to close off my airways! But I wanted to feel courageous, and not just when standing before a group of people. I wanted to have the courage to do what needed to be done—the kind of courage my dad has.

While our family was living in Latin America, Dad often piloted his own single-engine airplane. And as a prominent and well-known international banker with Citibank, he had a good reputation not only as a pilot but also as an honest man who was capable and trustworthy.

One day a minister from a local church came to Dad with an unusual request. "Mr. Wells," the minister said, "You are a good man who has served God in many ways. I have a major problem. I have prayed for guidance and have been led to you for help." Intrigued, Dad thanked the man and asked what he could do to help. The minister told Dad that he had just learned from one of their mission outposts in the jungle that a woman there was in desperate need of medical attention or she would surely die. She needed to be evacuated immediately.

Dad had been called upon often for charitable donations and assumed this was the case, so he assured the minister that he would gladly pay for the charter flight to bring her out. The minister quickly answered, "No, it's not the money that we need, it is *you*. Have you read the paper this morning?"

The only thing in the morning paper that had caught Dad's attention was news of an invasion by some dissident rebels from across the border. Had he missed something? The minister explained that because of the invasion, the government had grounded all civilian planes—*nothing* would be authorized. "You are a trusted friend of the government and I feel you can get permission to make the flight," the minister said.

Dad knew he needed to do whatever he could to help save the woman's life, so the day's business was set aside and Dad reached for the phone. First he called an old friend, the leader of the country's Civil Aviation Affairs. After being greeted warmly, he said, "My friend, I understand that all civil flights are grounded, but I need permission to fly my plane into the jungle to evacuate a woman who needs an emergency operation. Can you arrange that for me?"

After a few moments of silence, his friend replied, "It is very difficult to have to turn you down, but I am under orders. Please understand. Troops have orders to fire at any nonmilitary aircraft that even moves." Further pleadings didn't do any good. Dejected, Dad turned to the minister and related the conversation. The minister responded softly, "I already know all that. I am here because I feel guided that you are the only one who can save this poor woman's life."

Dad said a silent prayer, then picked up the phone and directly dialed another acquaintance, the military general in charge of the country's air force. The general was courteous but firm—he could not help. Dad then made one last call—to the president himself. He reached the president's personal secretary, who told Dad to hold while he made an attempt to get authorization for this one flight. But of course, the secretary returned, apologized that he was unable to interrupt the president who was in a tense meeting, and concluded by saying, "The woman will just have to die."

Unwilling to give up, Dad thought of one other thing. The main airport was crawling with troops ready to shoot down any civilian plane, but maybe, he thought, the air club with a grass runway on the opposite side of the city had been forgotten. He thought of a risky plan. As he and the minister drove to the club, Dad explained that they would take the club's green Stinson to make the flight. He had loaned the club the money to buy it and had been given permission to use it any time. This plane required no key—it was ready to fly the moment one turned on the master switch.

Arriving at the club, they saw about ten armed soldiers standing around the hangars. Dad recognized the officer in charge as one of the air force captains with whom he had flown as co-pilot. Glancing at the Stinson, Dad saw that it was untied and sitting unguarded. He whispered to the minister, "You walk to the far side of the plane, open the door, and get in—don't say a word."

Together they walked quickly to the plane and jumped in. Dad found the master switch, hit the starter, and the engine roared to life on the first try. The officer and the troops immediately came running, shouting something Dad couldn't hear over the engine. Dad slid open the window but kept the engine running. The officer gave Dad a signal to cut the engine by drawing his finger quickly across his throat. In reply, Dad wiggled his finger. The officer then raised his automatic pistol. Instead of backing down though, Dad made a toy pistol out of his left hand, and pointed it at the engine. With his right hand, he moved his index finger back and forth to say, "Don't shoot me—shoot the engine."

Unbelievably, the officer just stared at him and didn't shoot. The plane took off safely; they landed at the mission, picked up the critically ill woman, and flew back to the air club, where an ambulance was waiting. The woman's life was saved. The officer who didn't shoot was disciplined; but Dad subsequently apologized to him and to the president of Paraguay. Later, when he had a chance to speak with the officer, Dad asked him why he didn't shoot him that day. The officer said simply, "I was fully prepared to shoot you, my friend, but when you made the gesture to shoot the engine and not you, well, as a pilot myself, I just couldn't ruin a perfectly good engine." Determined to do the right thing, Dad found a way and found his courage.

Following your own inspiration and gut feelings is all part of pushing the comfort zone ever outward. Learning to listen to yourself and to value your own opinion is just as important, and often more important, than listening to others. Courage isn't just about heroics on the battlefield or strength in tragedy. It's also about breaking through limits and fears, including everyday kinds of fears like taking a chance, doing the hard things, or doing the right things.

## EXERCISING YOUR INSTINCTS

The "survival instinct" you were born with is there to be active, not passive. But sometimes it is buried under another very strong instinct . . . the instinct that makes you want to take the easy route—to sit back and do nothing instead of standing and doing something.

Courage is a lot like some of the muscles in the body—the ones that most of us don't even know we have because they are used so infrequently. Look at your triceps, for example. Triceps are one of the most underused muscles in the body. Yet strong triceps make for beautiful arms that don't "wiggle" when you wave. Of course the only way to build any muscle, including your triceps, is to exercise it. I can just hear the groans: "But exercise is hard. It takes time." True, but look at the rewards: a longer life, better sleep, fewer illnesses, greater strength. Developing the courage to leave your comfort zone is much like exercise, and the results are similar as well.

To be in shape, you have to get in shape. And that means work. You must visit the gym or go for that run or take that walk. Sitting around thinking about it does you no good. Likewise, to be comfortable outside your comfort zone, you have to live there, or at least visit often.

Consistent and *meaningful* exercise is the key. And don't forget meaningful. My husband is a physical therapist who owns a popular and reputable clinic. A woman called him recently begging for advice on how to flatten her stomach (most people would call the local gym for this kind of advice, but since she had been a patient at the clinic, she called there first). She said she had been doing sit-ups for ten years with nothing to show for it. My husband, sensing the problem immediately, asked her how many sit-ups she was doing daily. She responded proudly, "Ten sit-ups!" My husband kindly suggested that she needed to do more, a lot more, to see results.

Will ten sit-ups build muscle and take away the fat? Of course not. But what will? Doing sit-ups until fatigued—which means something like ten *sets* of ten a day—will build muscle. But to actually take away the fat that is covering up those abs, you need to participate in some form of aerobic exercise on a regular basis—three to five times a week, at least. It's simply not possible to target and remove fat from only one area of the body. You must work the whole body. And that's when things really start to happen—after consistent and meaningful exercise.

Many of us can easily come up with a number of excuses at one time or another to defend why we just can't find the time to work out or get in shape. When something is too hard—or if it is something we do not do well—we have a tendency to make excuses for not doing it. And if we can't find a suitable excuse for our inaction, we assign blame to someone or something else. By doing this, we take the fastest route back to our comfort zones.

## A FEW "TRICKS" TO GET YOU GOING

I've discovered that the first attempt to move outside my comfort zone takes the most courage. If I can find something else to get me started on a goal, it makes it easier to venture outside my zone. It also takes away the fear of plunging into what might be waist-high mud on the shores of my pond.

I especially like the "trick" that many people used during the 2002 Winter Olympics—held in my hometown of Salt Lake City—to meet people who were sharing in the Games with them. I call it "the Olympic pin trading phenomenon." Complete strangers found it easier to approach each other and step outside of their usual shyness if they had a shiny little pin in their hands. More often than not, a pin exchange turned into the beginning of a friendship, even if it was a short friendship. People weren't afraid to talk to each other if the conversation began with a pin exchange. Without this "tool," many people never would have left their comfort zones and met "friends" from Germany, England, Japan, Australia, or even Colorado, right across the state line. I heard from many Olympic volunteers that after sixteen days of pin trading, they felt much more confident talking to new people even *without* the use of Olympic pins.

Something else that makes it easier—and less frightening—to move outside my comfort zone is taking a friend along. It won't always happen, but when you do get the opportunity to do something hard that has been done before, find a pal to go with you. And go soon, too.

The sooner you go, the easier it will be, and the more

fun, too. It's much like the mass-event phenomenon described in a *Time* magazine article about the 2002 hit movie *Spider-Man.* "We yearn for mass events," writes Joel Stein. "Whereas movies and music once built an audience slowly, entertainment is now disposable, designed to gather a heterogeneous society together for one week and then fade away. . . . Nowadays, if you see an event movie after the first couple of weeks, you're not really a participant but an observer, a sociologist trying to discover what it was that everyone was so excited about" ("Blockbuster Summer," 20 May 2002, vol. 159, no. 20 72, 74–75). Read that quote again, and remember—it takes participation, *not observation,* to move outside of your comfort zone.

## NO EXCUSES

As you begin to venture out of the warm, relaxing waters of your comfort zone, remember that some things really *are* out of your control and things *can* go wrong. All of us have to accept that fact and deal with it. But, as hard as it may be to admit, you are the only one ultimately responsible for your life and what you get out of it. You are the only person in the world you have complete control over. Excuses will never make you successful, no matter how good that excuse might be.

We all have excuses. We all have something, or someone, we could blame when things go wrong in our lives. Granted, some excuses are more legitimate than others. But no matter the depth or magnitude of the obstacle, if you use it to let yourself off the hook or keep yourself from a good challenge, then you will harm only yourself. Just ask Jim Knaub. Ask Christopher Reeves or Helen Keller, Franklin D. Roosevelt or Beethoven, Stevie Wonder or any number of folks who might live right in your own neighborhood. These people have become greater by rising above and beyond their personal "excuses." In fact, I can think of only one group of people that has a really good reason for staying within the confines of their small circles. They are sumo wrestlers! They *lose* if so much as one toe steps outside of the circle before their opponent's. But the rest of us only stand to gain.

## REAL QUIET

In May 1998, while I was working at the Kentucky Derby, I saw firsthand a remarkable performance by the unlikeliest of characters to ever run at Churchill Downs. His name was Real Quiet and, as it turns out, he was perfectly named. Even though he's a horse, whose life hardly resembles any of ours, I wish more of us could be like him.

Real Quiet's story began in March 1995, when he was foaled at a bluegrass horse farm in Kentucky—a skinny little colt with crooked legs. With no one expecting racing greatness from him, he underwent surgery to straighten those legs with the hope that he would simply be able to walk well someday, maybe even run a little.

Engraved on his bridle was Real Quiet's endearing nickname: The Fish. You see, Real Quiet possessed one unique fishlike characteristic; if you looked at him head-on, he almost disappeared—just like some tropical fish. Bottom line, he just didn't look like a horse that could win many races, though his pedigree was certainly solid.

At the famous September Keeneland Sale in Kentucky, where the most promising colts are bought for hundreds of thousands of dollars, and even millions of dollars on the first or second day, The Fish waited to be sold. He was passed over on the first and second days. On the third day, there was still no sign of interest in Real Quiet. On the fourth day, not many pricey horses were left, and he was passed over once again. On the fifth and final day, one trainer saw something in this horse that made him look twice. Bob Baffert—a now-famous trainer who stormed onto the thoroughbred racing scene in 1996 with a near-win at the Kentucky Derby, and has since followed with many high-profile wins—picked up The Fish for a mere $17,000. That is nickels and dimes in the "Sport of Kings!"

In 1997, Real Quiet began racing. He won only twice in twelve career starts, but he had enough earnings to get him into the Kentucky Derby the following spring. There, he was the horse no one talked about or cared to photograph. When his more famous stable mate, the Derby-favorite Indian Charlie, would leave the barn, photographers and reporters followed him closely. When The Fish would leave seconds later, nobody wanted his picture. He was the ugly duckling, the "other" horse in Bob Baffert's stable.

Finally, the famous Churchill Downs trumpet blew, calling the horses to post. The gates flung open, and the field of fifteen horses burst onto the track, immediately looking for the best spot near the rail. I watched as this mass of power sped toward me, then curved away to speed down the backstretch. At that point it is too hard to tell how the horses are doing (unless you have a bird's-eye view like the commentators do). The track is immense and the pack of horses so tight that their numbers get lost. So we just listened to the announcer as he yelled out the moves of those in the lead.

As the horses neared the top of the stretch, I could see one horse taking the lead . . . and it wasn't any of the horses most of us had picked to win. It was the horse no one ever expected to race well, the skinny horse, the completely underestimated and ignored horse, perfectly named Real Quiet. But he was no longer in a quiet mood as he thundered down the stretch in front of 110,000 people at Churchill Downs. This $17,000 horse beat out the million-dollar babies for the red roses and a spot in history. As he stood in the winner's circle, cameramen zoomed in on the small brass plaque tacked to his bridle that read simply The Fish. Once an endearing nickname, it now stood as a proud reminder to all those associated with him of the power of a strong heart.

But The Fish's story doesn't end there. Two weeks later at the Preakness—the second "jewel" in horse-racing's elite Triple Crown Series—Real Quiet again showed the crowd what a $17,000, once crippled, underestimated horse could do as he snatched the $650,000 purse. With two of the jewels in his pocket, Real Quiet now had a real shot at winning the Triple Crown—a rare distinction very few horses in racing history can claim. Secretariat was one of those historic horses and Affirmed—the last horse to win the Triple Crown in 1978—was another. But at the Belmont (the final jewel) just three weeks later, Real Quiet ran a nail-biter of a race against his old nemesis Victory Gallop, who had placed second to Real Quiet in the last two races. In the photo finish, Victory Gallop was the winner by barely an inch or two. Real Quiet came within a nostril of a perfectly unbelievable Hollywood ending.

Real Quiet was never supposed to amount to much. Had he been human, he probably would have done something to sabotage himself, like compare himself to other thoroughbreds: "That horse went for a million dollars! I was bought for $17,000, so I must not be any good!" But Real Quiet succeeded because he's just a horse with an incredible heart. He can't compare, he can't underestimate himself, and he can't fear failure. All he knows how to do is look straight down the track in front of him, race with all his heart, and listen to the encouraging words of the jockey on his back—not the crowd, which may be saying "no you can't." And he knows that win or lose, he has a staff of trainers who will take good care of him, give him a bath when he's all done, feed him his favorite oat mixture, and then let him run in the pasture.

What and who are taking *you* for a ride? What type of support system or safety net is always there for you after a big race? Those are the two key elements we'll discuss in Steps 2 and 3. And after you've answered those two questions in depth, Step 4 will help you take a look at some of the specifics that are needed in order to challenge your comfort zone walls.

At that point you'll be anxious to challenge your comfort zone. After all, the pond can get real boring when the weather is hot and the air stagnant. Kissing one of those frogs out in the swamp might actually start to sound good if you know that the prize could bring a change of scenery, a little more adventure and spice to your life, and perhaps even help you fulfill one of your fondest dreams. Once outside you will find it's not as uncomfortable as you might have imagined. So pucker up!

*Step 2*

# IDENTIFY THE FORCES THAT ACTIVATE AND DEACTIVATE YOU

"How Do I Love Thee?
Let's Definitely Count the Ways
Before I Stick Out My Neck"

Chapter 4

# EXCUSES:
# THE NEGATIVE FORCES

Have you ever thought about or defined the factors that activate or *de*activate you when faced with an important— or sometimes just a basic—decision? Those things or people that either help start the fire or throw a huge bucket of water over the wood you were hoping to light? When do your own feelings tend to have greater power over your choices, and when do the feelings of others come into play? Which forces seem to propel you toward the edge of your comfort zone? Everyone has to be at least a little proactive in order to exist. We have to make sure our basic needs, such as food, shelter, and clothing are met for us and for those who depend on us. But what and/or who drives you to action beyond that? What and/or who builds or destroys the person inside of you? What elements cause you to act in such a way that you do things that go beyond the filling of basic survival needs?

Most people who are considering moving outside of their comfort zones can usually come up with a handful of excuses for not doing so: *But the frog is so unappealing!*

*What if I get a disease? It's just too hard wading out through the swampy water, getting all dirty and wet! What if the frog doesn't want to be kissed? It would take too much time to catch that little jumpy thing . . . and what guarantee do I have that it will turn into a prince anyway?* That's why it is important to recognize these excuses as *negative*—or *deactivating*—forces that will *prevent* you from broadening your comfort zone. Actually writing down these forces on paper and analyzing them will do a lot to help you feel good about broadening your zone. After reading this chapter and identifying your own deactivating forces, determine whether one of these forces is more dominant than the others and assign a number to each one in order of the most influential to the least. Four possible forces follow:

### 1. THE FEAR OF FAILURE

I remember watching the World Series in 1986 when the Boston Red Sox let the New York Mets take the series away from them. For those of you who might remember that game, you'll know I'm not exaggerating. Soon after the game, a reporter cornered Wade Boggs in a depressingly quiet dugout where he asked an unbelievably obvious question: "How do you feel?" Boggs was so despondent he couldn't even come back with a wisecrack and instead, his response was simple. "Losing hurts worse than winning feels good," he said slowly as he stared out onto the diamond filled with celebrating New York Mets fans and players.

Experiencing failure is such a devastating blow to the very core of how we feel about ourselves that we naturally want to avoid feeling that way again. When I fail (and believe me it's an ongoing occurrence) my initial reaction is embarrassment, and then I want to hide. Every time I mess up I feel as if I'm the only one that that particular thing could possibly happen to. Although that is my initial reaction, experience has taught me that I can't afford to waste time being down on myself. I can't afford it because dwelling on my failures doesn't bring me any closer to success. Getting past failure is an integral part of the success process.

I love to watch figure-skating events. When I view a competition on television, I'm fascinated by the leaps the skaters attempt. And I always find myself getting a little nervous when I see a skater building up for a jump and hear the announcer say something like, "She's attempting a triple-toe loop, a feat she has never before successfully landed in competition."

During one telecast of a figure-skating event, I heard an announcer say, just as one of the competitors fell to the ice, "It's not the fall, but the *reaction* to the fall that can be fatal!" What great wisdom! We can learn a great deal from those who publicly handle defeat and errors well. They get up, dust off the ice, and move on. Granted, some do carry on like little children by getting into fights and blaming everyone and everything around them for the failure. But it's the *good* sport that we can emulate in our own real-life mistakes and failures.

Understandably, failure is just not fun. And every one of us knows the pain, and sometimes the sheer despair, that accompanies failure. Somewhere during my own junior high and high school days of self-discovery, I learned for myself that those who win most often also tend to fail more regularly. I realized that if I never failed, it meant I hadn't set high enough goals. So I decided to focus on the goal itself and not the possibility that I was risking failure.

Anyone who has made a success of his or her life knows that failure is a *means to* success. In 1985, one of the biggest marketing fiascos to ever hit the shelves made a remarkable turnaround. Coca-Cola decided to change the formula of the world's number-one soft drink, making it sweeter and—so it seemed—closer in taste to its archrival, Pepsi. They called their new formula "New Coke." When "New Coke" was introduced, consumers immediately rebelled, refusing to buy it. But because of the Coca-Cola Company's quick reaction (company heads didn't sit around and wallow in self-pity), "Classic Coke" was reintroduced in a massive marketing campaign that had many experts wondering if the whole thing had actually been planned.

The ultimate about-face success of this marketing disaster seems to stem from the company's overriding philosophy of acknowledging mistakes, taking responsibility for them, and even recognizing the need for mistakes.

Sergio Zyman, the marketing executive behind the disastrous launch of "New Coke," left the company almost immediately after its failed release. Even so, he often consulted with the company and was eventually rehired and put in charge of global marketing. Why? When asked for an explanation by *Fortune* magazine, CEO Roberto Goizueta said, "We became uncompetitive by not being tolerant of mistakes. The moment you let avoiding failure become your motivator, you're down the path of inactivity. You can stumble only if you are moving" (as quoted in Patricia Sellers, "So You Fail. Now Bounce Back!" *Fortune,* May 1995, 48).

I love that quote: *You can stumble only if you are moving.*

In 1968, a brash but very talented eighteen-year-old swimmer predicted that he would win an unbelievable six gold medals at the Olympics in Mexico City. But Mark Spitz failed miserably in comparison to his own expectations. He won two gold medals as a member of the U.S. relay teams, swam dead last in the 200-meter butterfly, and placed second in the 100-meter butterfly (the event for which he held the world record). He was demoralized, but used his tremendous personal failure and humiliation to drive him forward instead of stalling him. It was his second-place finish that egged him on the most. He explained, "I thought about that race every day for four years. Because it was absolutely the worst thing that happened to me, I kept swimming another four years."

That additional four years took him to the 1972 Olympics in Munich, West Germany, where he swam into history as one of the modern era's greatest athletes, winning an unprecedented seven gold medals—four in individual events and three in relays. The reason we all recognize the name Mark Spitz is precisely because he had failed big, reacted even bigger, and *then* succeeded. What if he had quit altogether, thinking he would never have a better chance?

When I was in college, I heard baseball great and five-time Golden Glove recipient Dale Murphy speak to a crowd of about fifteen thousand people, and I'll never forget one small sentence he said. "When I'm in a slump, I keep swinging hard just in case I hit it." I have always remembered that: *When I'm in a slump, I keep swinging hard just in case I hit it.* Dale Murphy was one of the best all-around major leaguers in the 1980s for that reason. He had the perfect formula for life, as well as for success in baseball. Some give up, back off, get cranky, and start throwing bats, but he just kept his eye on the ball and swung hard time after time.

How high up does the fear of failure rank on your list of *de*activating factors? Do you remember the last time you backed down or backed out of something? Do you remember why? Was it the fear of failure? John Wayne, in character, was direct and to the point in his answer to failure. Right after punching a smart-mouth young man into the dirt, he drawled, "Kid, you'll be getting up after you've been knocked down all your life. Get used to it."

## 2. THE COST OF COMPARISONS

A second deactivating factor in the quest to move outside our comfort zones is comparison. How often do you underestimate or "ground" yourself because you don't feel that you measure up?

I first discovered my own tendencies to make comparisons when I was in high school. I ran the hurdles, which I loved doing at practice but not at meets—against real competition and in front of an audience. I was always a nervous wreck. I remember warming up right before one particular race. While trying to appear as casual as possible, I carefully looked over my competition. I saw one girl warming up on the blocks and thought, *Boy, her starts look powerful.* Then I looked over at another girl as she sprinted in spurts to loosen up. *She looks fast enough to be in the Olympics*, I thought. And then my eyes wandered to another as she glided over a couple of hurdles to make sure her rhythm was there. *Wow, she's smooth.* Suddenly I had convinced myself I was racing against Jackie Joyner-Kersee. I had blended my competitors into the world's greatest athlete and knew I didn't stand a chance.

The more I raced, the more I recognized what I was doing to myself. So I began to look inward for my competition, to focus on my own lane straight ahead and not turn my head to see the others. I discovered that I was my wor-thiest opponent. (No one knows me—and my weaknesses and strengths—better.) I soon began winning for a while. But then, injuries and musical interests steered me in other directions. Though I never became a track star, I valued the lesson I had learned on the field: looking at the com-petition instead of focusing on your own lane just slows you down and increases the likelihood that you will trip over a few hurdles.

Do you ever underestimate yourself? Do you say to yourself, "Nah, I couldn't do that." Often, people do this because they see someone else who *can* do the task at hand with ease and talent. One of the first rules of taking a trip outside your comfort zone is eliminating the compar-isons. They just weigh you down. When you compare, you lose all perspective of what you have going for you. And that's when you underestimate yourself. How can courage possibly grow where weeds of comparisons have taken over?

One of the saddest faces I have ever seen was that of my four-year-old son Jacob after his older sisters started proving how smart they were by asking each other simple addition questions. One turned to him and asked, "Do you know what 1 plus 36 is?" He didn't know. He came over to me wiping away great big tears. "I'm not smart, Mom. I'm not smart," he managed to whimper in between sobs. What was his "proof" that he wasn't smart? A sister who asked him a question he was too young to understand. But he concluded he wasn't smart because she knew the answer and he didn't. He was so demoralized he couldn't think straight. And his mind, of course, was too young to reason: "Hmmm, I'm four years old and she is six. She has just graduated from kindergarten, so of course her brain is a little more developed and trained than mine. But that doesn't mean I won't eventually understand the principles of addition. In the meantime, I'll concentrate on throwing that baseball a little straighter." He just wanted me to hold him and tell him over and over that his brain was getting bigger every day and that some day it would do all kinds of amazing things, especially if he kept telling it that it could. He started to feel a little more courageous.

Comparisons tend to go around in circles, even twisting and turning on occasion. For example, I may see someone who has a talent I want for myself—let's say it's my next-door neighbor, Susan, who is an excellent gardener. Instead of stretching myself a little and learning to grow a few basic plants, I may simply sit at my window and look out at Susan's garden, comparing the beauty of her yard to my own neglected and overgrown rosebushes. At the same time, it's quite possible that Susan, while down on her knees in the garden, is looking over at Amy—the neighbor across the street—and berating herself for not doing more to excel professionally and thus land a great job like Amy's. In the meantime, Amy is gazing out her window as she gets ready for work and soon begins comparing herself to Jackie, who is out playing with her children, and wishes she could be more of a fun mom. Instead of *learning* from each other or *admiring* each others' talents, we are all sitting around doing nothing but focusing on the things we don't do well. Making comparisons is just like being a spectator who is completely out of the game and thus has no control over its outcome. When we switch the gears over to *admiring and learning,* we place ourselves in the game—giving ourselves a chance to actually do some of the scoring.

I had worked with ESPN just one year when I was

assigned to be part of the coverage for the World Alpine Championships in Vail, Colorado. For two weeks I had been on skis, and I was ready for a change of pace . . . *perhaps a little tennis,* I thought. There was a tennis club just across the street from my lodgings, so I begged a friend to meet me there on my day off for a quick match. At the club, we were given our court assignment—one all the way at the end. As we walked through the heavy plastic curtains that keep the tennis balls inside the court, our jaws dropped.

Chris Evert—*the* Chris Evert—was on the court, one of the greatest and most respected tennis players in the world.

As we quietly sat down on the bench, she looked over to us and said, "I'm sorry, we'll be off in a minute." The two of us, almost in unison, said, "Go ahead. Take your time." It's not too often you get a private showing of such great talent. But all too soon she told us the court was ours, and she went over to get her things. I expected her to leave, but instead she and her partner sat down and started drinking some water. There was no way I wanted to play in front of *her! Why didn't she leave?* I wondered. I slowly laced up my sneakers, slowly took off my warm-ups, got a drink, looked for just the right tennis balls, and still she sat.

My partner and I had stalled about as long as we could, but finally we each took a side of the court. At that moment, I could almost imagine what it must feel like to stand on Court Central at the French Open finals. I was that nervous. All I could think about was what Chris Evert would think of my practically nonexistent tennis skills. But she probably wasn't even thinking of us at all, and most likely had no idea that she was ruining our tennis outing.

Just as we started lobbing the ball to each other, she picked up her stuff and left, giving us a smile as she walked out. Whew, what a relief! Later, though, I nearly kicked myself for being so in awe that I couldn't have asked her one question that would've helped me better my own game . . . maybe something like "how do you know when to approach the net?" She might have even shown me.

The next year, I was sent to Florida to spend two days with the young tennis marvel Monica Seles (at the time, she was fifteen years old and ranked sixth in the world). I again nearly let comparisons ruin a great opportunity to learn. As we were taping Monica doing her usual morning workout, my producer suggested that I grab a racket and hit a few balls back and forth with her. Immediately I thought of my fears. *She's one of the best in the world! She'll laugh at me! She'll think it's a complete waste of her time! She'll demolish me!* But then I remembered how I hadn't been too happy with my scared-rabbit reaction to Chris Evert, so I decided to be brave, to forget my fears, and to grab the opportunity to play with the best.

*Play* is probably too strong a word for what we did out on the court . . . maybe "toyed with" or "knocked a few balls around" sums it up better. But I had a great time dashing all over my side of the court and hitting the ball back as hard as I could to Monica, who looked like a cat having fun with a mouse. After about fifteen minutes, I was huffing and puffing so I told her I'd give her a break. She was so sweet. I immediately liked this girl who was willing to humor me. Since I had been trying so hard, I just had to ask her out of curiosity, "So, at what percentage level did you play me? Seventy-five percent, maybe?" She laughed and said (in front of our cameras), "Actually about

30 percent." Okay, I was chagrined, but that was over-shadowed by the fact that in fifteen minutes I learned from one of the best instead of safely standing on the sidelines carefully guarding my ineptness out on the court. She did make me feel better, though, by adding that there was one cross-court burner I hit that reminded her of Steffi Graf! Now, that's the part I'll choose to remember instead of all my other weaknesses.

How much of a force in your life is the need to compare? And when you do compare, are you learning or self-destructing?

## 3. THE FEAR OF REJECTION

The fear of rejection is the primary reason that keeps a boy from asking out a girl. Why? Because rejection is a statement. It says "I don't like you enough to be with you or accept you." Though closely associated with failure, rejection is even more personal. It is an attack on our inner core. Failure is generally objective in nature. Having failed, you might say one of the following: "I wasn't fast enough," "I didn't do well on the test," "I was outbid by another contractor," or "I made too many mistakes during the piano solo." But rejection is typically *subjective,* dealing more with other people's opinions about you. Feeling rejected, you might say to yourself: "I was not elected to office *because they didn't like me*"; "I was turned down for a job for which I have credentials *because they didn't like me*"; "I was not accepted into a club *because they didn't like me*"; or "He divorced me *because he didn't love me*." Rejection makes us feel worthless, and unless we can quickly shift our focus back to those who *do* care and all the reasons why we *are* of great worth, it can swiftly suck us into a quicksand trap.

My mother-in-law and father-in-law were both school-teachers in Idaho until they retired about seven years ago. Theirs was a constant challenge not only to educate the children in their classes but to encourage them and help them through their struggles. But some struggles are very quiet and hidden, and no one knows when serious help is needed until it is sometimes too late. The powerful and self-destructive nature of rejection is perhaps the most hurtful of all negative/deactivating forces.

On a quiet evening, just half a block away from my in-law's home, a thirteen-year-old girl was found hanging under the bleachers—a suicide blamed on a broken, rejected heart. She had been teased to the point of hope-lessness about her weight and her poverty. My in-laws said she was a bright girl with many capabilities, but the rejection was apparently more than she could bear.

How do we prevent rejection from destroying our very lives? How do we turn our backs on rejection? We'll cover that more in detail later, but here we'll acknowledge it as a real *de*activating and *de*moralizing aspect of everyone's lives. It can range from a husband who walks in one night and tells his wife he no longer loves her to a trivial thing (in comparison) like being stood up for a date. It can take the wind right out of your sails for a day or two, or even a few years. But rejection of any voltage can be—and has been—defeated.

My experience with rejection will seem trivial com-pared to most. No matter where rejection comes from, however, it still hurts, still causes self-doubt, and still leaves the rejected feeling completely alone in the world.

There were many times during my year as Miss America that I wanted to quit altogether. No matter where I went, there was always someone who wanted nothing more than to point out my faults—from my hair to my nose to my opinions to whether or not I had any real talent. Even my religious beliefs were under attack. And I thought we lived in a country of "political correctness!" I learned all about mass rejection in the first few weeks of being "America's sweetheart."

One incident—which, in hindsight, is also rather amusing—in particular was quite effective in letting out any air that might have been filling up my head. The Outdoor Advertising Association of America had requested my participation in a national marketing study to see how effective billboards were. First, an informal poll would be taken in different metropolitan parts of the country to see if anyone knew who the new Miss America was. Then billboards—with a huge picture of me and a caption that simply read, "Sharlene Wells, Miss America 1985"—would be placed in those same areas. After two months, the poll would be taken again to see if name recognition had jumped and by how much.

Besides using my picture and name, the association asked me to actually take part in the polling. It was part of the publicity, I suppose. I was taken to downtown Los Angeles where one billboard would be placed, and there I stood on a corner for two hours, stopping people at random. With a picture of the top ten finalists in hand, I showed the photo to whomever I stopped and asked the person if he or she could pick out who won Miss America. Of course I didn't identify myself, and no one even asked. For the first hour and forty-five minutes, no one picked me out of the group photo. They kept pointing to all the other girls, not even hesitating when passing me up. Finally, one of the last people to be polled looked at the picture and quickly pointed to me in the photo, saying, "Yeah, she won." I was thrilled that someone thought I could win! But before I could offer my congratulations and identify myself, he moved his finger on down the picture to another girl and said, tapping her photo with confidence, "But *she* should have won." Ouch.

Right after that very interesting and sometimes bumpy ride as Miss America, I returned to college to finish up the two years I had left. You might guess that I would be fairly confident, fresh from a year of being in the spotlight. You might even assume that there would be young men lining up to ask me out. But the reality was this: now that I was a "public figure," anyone who wanted to could write letters to the editor saying I was a ditzy blond. They could call in to radio talk shows and make up stuff about me, or draw cartoons with me as the point of the joke. I wore baseball caps to class to avoid being noticed. I genuinely thought people would openly make fun of me.

And as for the men lining up to ask me out? Well, to begin with, my boyfriend dumped me for another girl about four months after I won. And then when I did get back, all was very quiet on the social front. The year following my stint as Miss America was one of the lowest periods of self-esteem in my life because I felt rejected and unloved . . . except by Mom and Dad, of course.

As a reporter I often have to ask people for interviews. Usually I have to beg. Since 1995, I've been assigned "Millionaire's Row" at the Kentucky Derby, where it is my job to interview a celebrity on our live broadcast every fifteen minutes or so. When celebrities say no, they can sometimes be a bit snobby about it. Several have simply ignored me. Others have politely turned down my request. On a particularly bad day, after multiple rejections, I asked Walter Cronkite—a true role model and probably the biggest celebrity there—for an interview. He told me he would be honored to do one. That erased the disappointment of all the other rejections. At that moment I could certainly understand why Sally Field blurted out enthusiastically when she won the Oscar in 1984, "You like me! You *really* like me!" It is a thoroughly exhilarating feeling to be accepted, recognized, and most especially, to be liked. It makes you feel like you can do anything!

The emotions that accompany rejection are quite the opposite but equally powerful. For a time—and that depends on how long you allow it to be so—you feel like you can do *nothing*.

How much value do you attach to your rejections? How long do you allow them to affect you?

## 4. BEING OVERBURDENED, OVERSHADOWED, AND OVERWORKED

There will be times when your current life demands are so great that to even *think* about doing anything else is laughable. Who wants *more* stress? Being overwhelmed can be a huge *de*activating force, keeping you from doing the things you would really like to try. On occasion, it can become an excuse—or a crutch—you use so you don't feel bad about not doing something.

The overwhelming demands of daily routines can often be enough to keep many of us trudging along in a ditch instead of climbing up and out where we can see more clearly. As a mother of four young children, I could use all twenty-four hours in the day to just stay on top of the needs of my family and home. It's safe to bet that most mothers feel overwhelmed at least 50 percent of the time.

At my house, for example, when my children were

very young, I never knew exactly when the day would start. It might have been at 2 A.M., when my three year old came running in saying, "A rabbit's trying to take my hot chocolate!" Or it could have been a blessed three hours later with a crash in the kitchen—the five year old is looking for the marshmallows. These days, I get more sleep, and if all goes well throughout the night—no scary dreams, ear infections, bathroom trips, and so on—I can usually make it out of bed by 6 A.M., just in time for the morning scramble of getting the kids dressed, finding the homework, and practicing the piano. Thankfully, I have a husband who fixes breakfast for all of us while I keep the kids on task. Although some relief comes with getting three of them out the door, I know that the most destructive of my four children is still in the house!

The rest of the day is really one adventure after another. I usually spend the morning cleaning up spills—a whole jug of Welch's grape juice on the kitchen floor can really slow down your morning—scraping up messes, and redistributing clutter. The hours seem to speed by. Just when I think I can slow down a bit, it's time to pick up my kindergartner, who more than once has had to call me in tears to ask where I am. Oh, those half days go by so fast!

During naptime I try to run to the computer to work on my professional projects. Then it's back to being teacher/janitor as soon as my son wakes up. Fortunately, I really *do* like being a mom (maybe because my children are so great!) and I wouldn't give it up for anything. But without a doubt, there are many frustrating moments, especially because of the many unfinished things that weigh on me. Being a mother is all about dealing with interruption.

I have a favorite cartoon that captures the essence of feeling overwhelmed. There is a picture of a cat that looks like he just touched a light socket, with hair straight up on end. The caption reads:

*I have gone to look for myself*
*If I should return before I get back,*
*Keep me here!*

How can any of us even *think* about leaving our comfort zones when there is plenty of work to do right inside of them? When you're overwhelmed, you feel tired—mentally, as well as physically. And when you're tired, you can't even begin to think of taking a trip somewhere, let alone a trip outside your comfort zone. When your well is dry, it's very difficult to think of ways to fill it.

So, let's review two of the ways we can overcome these feelings and get motivated to expand ourselves and our comfort zones. The first thing you can do is recognize that visiting the area just outside your comfort zone doesn't necessarily mean you have to "do" something. Challenging your comfort zone is first and foremost a state of mind. Think of it as an adventure of the mind—until you have the time to do something about it. If your mind is already *open* to new adventures or the thought of trying something hard, then it will be that much easier to do so when you really are in a position to devote the time to challenge yourself.

As a parent of young children, for example, the best thing I can do is to care for my children. I don't have to take on new and great projects if time won't allow. Instead, I can turn my thoughts—and thus my actions—to meeting my children's needs well now so I have time later to begin inching my way out of my comfort zone. For now, I just focus on my family's immediate needs and filling them well; but I do "daydream" about the challenges I'll take on once the children are *all* in school. For instance, right now with my youngest in preschool, I have taken on one small challenge—getting a master's degree *one class at a time.* It will take me a total of four years to get this degree, but by the time I have it, all the children will be in school all day and I will be ready for a new adventure outside my comfort zone. Besides, I've learned that by taking on something difficult just a little at a time and focusing on what's in front of me, I hardly notice when I've traveled a good mile outside those zone boundaries.

The second way to overcome feelings of discomfort, stress, and heavy burdens is to control your perspective of life and its challenges. The first time I scuba dived to forty feet, I had to control which perspective I would concentrate on so I could survive the experience! It wasn't until we dropped to the ocean floor and I looked *up* that a wave of fear swept over me. Looking up at all that water overhead—an amount of water I had never seen *with me in and under it*—gave me the feeling of looking over the edge of a skyscraper. I thought to myself, *don't look up; just look at all the pretty fish swimming around you. Pretend you're in a little pool. Concentrate on the fish!* It worked, and I was just fine. When it came time to head to the surface, we ascended gradually and specifically, not all at once. To keep from feeling overwhelmed, I had to look at what was directly in front of me and not at the enormity of everything around me. And let me tell you, it made all the difference, just as it does in daily life.

Focus on the task at hand, and you can get through anything. Don't let all the demands you are feeling over-burden you to the point of being paralyzed. Set aside any thoughts of what others might be doing, and how they might be doing it, and most especially, bury your expectations. Just do what you can do *when* you can do it. Take pride in the fact that you are at least moving. You *can* do it!

*But on the Other Hand,*
*I Hear There's Royalty on*
*One of Those Lily Pads*

Chapter 5

# POSSIBILITIES:
# THE POSITIVE FORCES

Now that we've gotten over the fact that frogs are sticky, beady-eyed, and all-around unappealing, what's next? Is there really royalty under that slimy green coat? Perhaps! The next step in expanding the boundaries of your pond is to determine the *positive* forces that *act*ivate or propel you in successful directions if you so choose. Following are five forces that can move you to action:

## 1. THE DESIRE TO BE HAPPY

Several years ago ABC aired a program called "The Mystery of Happiness" and revealed the results of an interesting poll. Fifteen hundred adults were asked if they had just one wish for their children—such as wealth, high intelligence, a successful career, or an overall happy life—what would it be? A happy life outpolled all the other choices combined ("The Mystery of Happiness," ABC Special Report, John Stossel reporting, 22 January 1998). The report went on to demonstrate that the desire to be happy is our greatest activating factor. It urges us to keep seeking, keep pushing, or keep doing whatever we have to in order to find happiness and keep it.

The pursuit of happiness, an unalienable right in the United States, means many things to many people. In an interview with Barbara Walters in the mid-1990s, Barbra Streisand was asked why she was auctioning off so many of the precious keepsakes and furniture she had accumulated over a long and successful career. "I want to simplify my life," was all she said. Barbra Streisand had moved beyond the need for awards or possessions to make her happy, and instead was finding peace in focusing on the more meaningful aspects of her life, such as relationships.

While the desire to be happy *can* potentially move you toward positive action, it can also propel you to do things that might not be too wise at certain points in your life. You should always be careful when you begin to think you'll be happy once you have all your wants met. Thinking, *"I'll be happy once I'm driving my new car around* or *once I buy that new outfit* or *once I'm the head of the company"* is not beneficial—especially if you don't have the money to buy a new car or aren't in the position to move up in the company.

In 1991 my husband, Bob, and I toured Egypt. On one particular afternoon, while shopping at a crowded outdoor bazaar, my husband struck up a conversation with a shopkeeper. They both kept looking at me and talking back and forth. Because I was already bargaining for a scarf and didn't want to miss the opportunity to purchase it, I didn't go over to join in their conversation. Soon, however, Bob joined me, still chuckling from his chat with the man. He explained that this sweet Egyptian man had made him an offer . . . for *me.* I was intrigued. "Oh, what did he offer you?" I asked. "Five hundred camels," he said with awe.

Bob had studied in the Middle East for six months and was well aware that five hundred camels was indeed a significant amount—one to at least consider. I, on the other hand, was not impressed. "So, what did you say?" I urged, a little concerned by how impressed he was with the thought of five hundred camels. "I told him it was indeed a huge offer, but that he couldn't buy you for any amount of camels." Bob smiled, knowing he had succeeded in ruffling my "women-are-not-just-subservient-toys-to-be-bartered-with" feathers.

Things (or in this case camels) really don't matter as much as people. If someone walked up to you and said, "I'll trade you this brand new mansion for your daughter," you'd laugh in his face. But many of us spend so much time and energy on material things that we are literally forsaking those very relationships we wouldn't trade the world for.

The desire to be happy is a powerful one—one that can activate you to step out of your comfort zone in order to achieve it. If your personal pride can be subdued, the desire to be happy in a relationship can help you learn how to do difficult things, such as saying "I'm sorry" and being willing to compromise. The desire to be happy can push you to be self-sufficient and independent and financially secure, so that your family's well-being isn't tied to anyone else. The desire to be happy with yourself can encourage you to learn to deal with failure, accept and work with your shortcomings, and celebrate your strengths. The desire to be happy can send you on a path of strengthening relationships, learning more about your spiritual nature, and making the changes necessary to put first things first. Sometimes you may think you're choosing a path toward happiness but soon find that the path actually leads away from that contented destination. In such a case, the best you can do is to make correct decisions that will help you get back on the right path.

When I chose one path in particular in my life, many people wondered about my state of mind. They thought I had chosen the wrong path, and to be quite honest, I questioned my own decision . . . for a few seconds. I chose a path that left behind my $250,000-a-year job for a much more difficult job that paid nothing—being a mom. After working full time for ESPN for seven years, it was easy to decide that my very young family needed me more and I needed them more. I really hadn't traveled much after my first daughter was born because ESPN had been extremely considerate of my wish to not be on the road much, but I no longer wanted to be committed to anyone or anything else other than the two most important people in my life. My oldest child was three at that time and my youngest was one; and today we have added two more reasons for happiness to the brood—another little girl and our only boy.

Occasionally there are times when I miss the excitement and variety of my old assignments: the red clay courts at the French Open, the sleek sailing boats of the America's Cup, the crisp fall afternoons of college football. But almost as instantly as those thoughts pop into my head, other thoughts replace them, such as the unsurpassable snapshots of how my children share their love and their joy. There's nothing, and I mean *nothing,* that comes close. Nothing I've ever done, nowhere I've ever gone, no amount of money I've ever made, no success I've ever achieved is even a close second. Being a mom is the best thing I've ever done, and it's also the hardest. But then again, what is the old saying? Anything worthwhile always is hard.

We all eventually discover or *re*discover that, believe it or not, happiness has nothing to do with things. It has to do with strong and meaningful relationships—relationships with oneself, with others, and with God. The desire to be happy can make you crazy sometimes as you try to figure out the exact pathway to happiness. Many things will tempt you with the promise of happiness, when in fact they really provide only temporary pleasure. But isn't it silly to put all of your efforts and resources into something *temporary?* If the desire to be happy is truly strong enough, then each of us can and will leave our comfort zones in the direction of relationships that will make us better people. We will agree to go to marriage counseling, to stop drinking so much alcohol, to make more time for the family, to hug our children and say, "I love you" . . . and we'll do it *all the time.* People change difficult habits every day in order to do what it takes to truly be happy.

## 2. THE DESIRE TO BE THE BEST

Why does competition exist? It's such a bad thing, *isn't it?* Wouldn't we all be better off living in a world where no one was better than anyone else, in anything? A world where we were all encouraged to stay the same and not do anything that might make us think we have greater talent than anyone else?

In a small town a number of years ago, many parents met together and decided that their children were better off playing Little League baseball without the competition factor. They wanted their children to play for the fun of it! It sounded like a great idea, everyone just playing ball and not really worrying about who was ahead. It was fun to be outside on a beautiful day, standing around hitting the ball to each other. On the first day of implementing this idea, the parents learned a valuable lesson about the symbiotic relationship of "fun" and "competition." After two innings of baseball the way the parents envisioned it, the kids gradually started migrating to the sandlot across the street, where pretty soon they got their own game underway—a game in which they could keep score. The children really did want to know who was winning . . . that's what made it exciting and fun! That's what made it a *game.*

I believe in competition because it drives individuals to reach a little higher than before. Inner competition—competing against yourself, trying to do better than your last personal best—is the toughest competition of all, because your opponent knows your weaknesses as well as you do! Competition tends to make people better than they were before. It may even make you better at a certain skill than the person next to you; just don't get confused and think that means you are of more worth than that person.

The desire to be the best can drive you to do the hard things. Right before the 1992 Olympics, I spent a couple of days at Dynamo Gym in Oklahoma City, where then Olympic hopeful Shannon Miller worked out. We were actually doing a special on the coaches that were headed to the Olympics and how they helped make Olympic dreams come true. During the course of those two days I interviewed Shannon's coach, Steve Nunno, and several others, including Shannon, about high-level coaching. To be quite honest, I don't remember much about what was said. But I do remember what I saw. I saw Shannon doing handstands and working on balance during "downtime," when the other gymnasts were lying on the mat resting. I saw Shannon do ten dismounts off the beam to everyone else's three or four. She quietly did more than the others. When she saw the others resting, she didn't join them.

At that time Shannon was unknown, but it was obvious that her desire to be the best kept her stepping out of her comfort zone (and I mean literally—gymnastics is a physically and mentally grueling sport!). I filed my impressions away and was not too surprised when she was a two-time Olympic silver medalist in 1992, the world all-around champion in 1993 and 1994, and the Olympic all-around gold medalist in 1996. She is the most decorated gymnast in American history because she had the desire to be the best. If that aim for excellence isn't there, it doesn't happen. You don't just accidentally achieve excellence.

All during my teenage years, I kept a sign above my bed that read:

*He who aims at excellence, will at least achieve mediocrity.*

*He who aims at mediocrity will fall far short of it.*

It's pointless to even enter a competition unless winning is your aim. Winning should be your aim in all of your preparations and in all of your thoughts and visualizations. Good sportsmanship, as well as honorable reactions to loss, should also be part of that preparation.

I think we all want to be number one. In the seventeen years I've been in sports broadcasting I have never heard anyone yell out, "We're number two!" That's because it's not good enough. I recall our crew being at a high school football game when the team we were covering finally broke a three-year losing streak. When we pointed the camera at the delirious players, what did they do? They yelled, "We're number one! We're number one!" as they ran all over the field. We're number one? Number one of what?

Those players were number one to those who mattered most to them. The team had finally won a game, and it was all worthwhile. There were no players around more acquainted with rebounding after failure than those seniors. In that, they were the best. For the seniors who failed all three years, yet continued in their daily practices, it wasn't the win that sent them scurrying around the field giving hugs to everyone. It was knowing that they hadn't quit just before the big win. It was knowing that because they had stuck it out through those years of drought, with absolutely nothing in the win column, they could *eventually* do anything.

The desire to be the best, even *your* best, is a powerful catalyst. Mediocrity brings nothing but disappointment to the table *unless* excellence was the true aim. Then, and only then, is there the dignity and pride of having at least tried.

## 3. THE DESIRE TO MAKE A DIFFERENCE

"Who stands still stands in his own way" is a motto for people who are activated by the desire to make a difference. These people, when activated by a cause that personally affects them, or when they truly believe that their involvement will mean the difference between success and failure, will do anything for those reasons alone. After all, most of us find it a lot easier to leave our comfort zones when we are confident we are needed. Being needed is a significant reward in and of itself. Helping others not only feels good, it's also good *for you*.

In May of 1998, the Institute for the Advancement of Health in New York City released a study that came as no surprise. A survey involving 3,300 volunteers found that 95 percent of the respondents experienced significant reductions in stress after doing some type of "helping" act. Also, many related that they had fewer colds, headaches, and backaches when they were serving others. They also reported improved eating and sleeping habits, as well as less pain from chronic conditions, such as arthritis. Allan Luks, director of the institute, compared the feeling of euphoria that volunteers experienced when helping others to the endorphin-induced feeling of the "runner's high." Luks calls this feeling the "helper's high," and claims that it relieves stress and raises self-esteem (see *The Healing Power of Doing Good,* N.Y.: Fawcett Columbine, 1992). Most people who serve others will attest to those results.

But is this "helper's high" the reason *why* people set out to make a difference in their community, their state, their country, even their world? I do not imagine that people methodically look at the circumstances and conclude that they will feel better about themselves if they join in. People who serve generally just see a need and have a burning desire to be part of the solution. Subconsciously, perhaps, these people recognize the opportunity to be *great* to someone else. And let's face it . . . when you feel *great* about making a difference, you feel great about yourself in general!

People with a desire to make a difference leave their comfortable and safe homes and venture out among those who might be in very different circumstances. They leave their comfortable worlds of relatively good health and mingle among the sick. They leave their comfortable freedom and visit with society's pariahs behind bars. And sometimes they just stop everything they're doing because someone, even a stranger, needs help.

I needed this kind of help one autumn afternoon as I flew over the handlebars of my bike. Speeding down a hilly road, the bright sun prevented me from seeing a small pothole in the road. Caught completely unaware, I was catapulted to the side of the road. This was back in the days when helmets had not quite caught on with the masses; because I wasn't wearing one, it was my head, shoulders, and thighs that softened the blow for the rest of my body. Fortunately, even though I knew I was pretty scraped up, I could tell that I was basically okay. Well, okay except for the fact that I couldn't see too well. Everything looked white.

Almost immediately I heard a man yell from his car, "Hey, are you okay?" With my back to him, and as I sat on the ground, I waved that I was okay. The next thing I knew, he was looking in my face and asking again, "Are you really okay?" I laughed, embarrassed by what must have been a comical scene, and said, "Yeah, I'm fine. I just live a few blocks from here. Thanks." Without arguing with me, he said that his family was in the car and they would be happy to take my mangled bike and me back to my home. I remember getting in the car and talking to all these people I couldn't really see because of all the white spots in front of my eyes.

After delivering me home, he asked if someone was there to take me to get my cuts stitched up (I had a whole bunch, and things were a little bloody). I replied that my younger sister was there but that I didn't have time to get stitches because I had to pick up my parents at the airport in an hour. They were getting home from a two-week trip and I had promised them I'd be out in front of the baggage claim. Well, this good Samaritan then told me that I would not be going to the airport to get my parents, but that *he* would. He assured me that he would greet them at the gate and let them know that I was okay. Still in a daze, I knew he was right and gratefully accepted his offer to serve.

My sister then took me to the medical center, my rescuer went to the airport, and all I can remember is a big white spot covering his face. (It turns out that the white spots were an indication of a mild concussion. I was stitched up and began seeing normally by the next day.) I may not remember his name or what he looked like, but the details of his actions have never left my memory. In fact, his desire to make a difference is something I remember on the occasions I am faced with my own opportunities to make a difference, and especially an *extra* difference like this man going to the airport.

Martin Luther King said, "We can all be great, because we can all *serve*." Now, it may not be greatness that people who serve are really after. But people who serve feel their lives have purpose and meaning. And, as a by-product, their service earns admiration, respect, love, and greatness.

In 1994 I received a letter that told of a simple country doctor who continually left his comfort zone—certainly not for any monetary reward, but because he knew he might possibly be the one to make a difference. Dr. J. P. Weber practiced medicine for fifty-two years. During this time he often risked his life to help those who were ill or suffering.

In 1932, for example, he needed to cross the Snake River in Hells Canyon to care for a child who was sick with scarlet fever. The ferryboat was resting on the Oregon side of the river, and its operator was out of town. Dr. Weber, who lived in Idaho, tied his medical bag to his waist, climbed up to the ferry cable, wrapped his legs and arms around it, and worked his way across the river.

Earlier in his medical career, when he was an intern at a Chicago hospital, Dr. Weber often treated immigrant families. One family he knew of lived on a fire escape—that's right, *on* the fire escape, not in the building—twenty-six floors up. Dr. Weber knew the mother was expecting a baby "any time." One late night he felt impressed to check on the family and the expectant mother. When he arrived he looked up and saw the family motioning to him, as if they knew he was coming. The mother was in labor. The front door to the building was locked, and Dr. Weber could not arouse anyone to open it. So he did what he could with what he had, despite the fear and tiredness he likely felt at that late hour. He used a rope to gain access to the fire escape and began climbing up the steps. He was eighteen floors up when he discovered that about five stories of the fire escape were missing! That portion of the fire escape had simply been removed. He tried again to attract the attention of someone inside the building but could not. So he tied his medical bag to his back and literally climbed the side of the building by grabbing hold of drainpipes and railings and window ledges, until he reached the bottom rung of the next portion of the fire escape. When he got to the twenty-sixth floor he met this family, who lived on two mattresses that were spread across the steps of the fire escape. A weary Italian mother, with Dr. Weber's help, delivered the baby there.

In the late 1920s Dr. Weber delivered another baby, this one the small boy of an impoverished family named Trout. Dr. Weber felt a strong attachment to this little boy named Eddie and even asked Mrs. Trout if he could adopt the boy and save him from the inevitable suffering this poor family would encounter. As the years went by, Dr.

Weber continued to ask Mrs. Trout about her son: "Are you going to give me my boy today?" He would ask.

Then, one day in December 1936, Dr. Weber received a phone call from Mrs. Trout. Eddie, now seven years old, had been hit by a drunk driver while attempting to cross a street. His little body had been thrown into a vacant lot by the impact of the crash, a distance of perhaps fifty feet. The doctor at Kooskia, where the family now lived, had refused to care for the boy because he considered him to be a hopeless case and because he knew the family couldn't pay.

The touching letter recounts what happened next: "Dr. Weber immediately drove to Kooskia, almost going off the icy, narrow road into the Clearwater River in the process. When he got to Kooskia, there was Eddie, this boy he loved so, lying in the snow, his brains streaming out into the snow and gravel. Dr. Weber loaded Eddie and his parts onto a stretcher and carried him to the family's home. He spent that night picking the gravel out of Eddie's brain and then closing the tiny skull. Dr. Weber lived with [Eddie's] family for weeks, doctoring Eddie back to health. Mrs. Trout told the doctor that the family didn't have a bed for him to sleep on. 'That's all right,' said Dr. Weber, 'I want to lie here and watch him.' This he said as he stretched out across the foot of the boy's bed. When he got up during the nights to check on Eddie, he often would inadvertently step on mice. . . .

"Eddie died in 1989 at the age of 60. Unfortunately, he was retarded due to the injuries he suffered in the accident. Dr. Weber never asked the Trout family for any payment for any of the work he did for them. (Mr. Trout was a very unprosperous prospector). Nor did the doctor ever ask the government for any reimbursement of his expenses or labor in caring for the Trouts (this I know because I have searched the indigency claim records carefully). It was all done from love" (letter in author's possession).

Dr. Weber died in 1976 at the age of eighty-eight. He left an estate worth less than $20,000.

Tom Weber, Dr. Weber's son, concluded his heartfelt letter by explaining that his father was certainly not a saint, but that he was just like the rest of us. His drive to perform his duties as a doctor, no matter how difficult, came from the activating desire to serve and make a difference, not to accumulate wealth.

## 4. THE DESIRE TO BE DIFFERENT

Moving from home to home and country to country was a way of life for my family, although I never got used to it. No matter how "experienced" I became at being the new girl, I was always anxious about what I might or might not find in the new area. Would I make new friends? Would I make the team? Perhaps the scariest move for me came when we moved *back* to America in the middle of my junior year of high school. After spending about twelve years of my young life in South America, I experienced "culture shock" in the United States, of all places!

The biggest concern for my sisters and me upon arriving in our new hometown was to determine what was "in." Like most teenagers, we figured that we could hardly be accepted if we were caught wearing non-trendy clothing. After about three days of investigating the local fashion industry, my youngest sister thought she had discovered exactly what was hip to wear. We were all sitting around the table eating breakfast that morning when my little sister walked in looking like she had just crawled out of bed. Her hair was "teased" out about five inches in all directions, she had freshly ripped holes in her jeans, together with the oldest-looking T-shirt she owned, and she was wearing sandals (even though it was snowing outside). She looked absolutely homeless. My mom casually reminded her that she needed to get ready for school or she would be late. Well, my sister immediately became defensive and announced that she *was* perfectly ready for school.

When we all raised our eyebrows, she said in her most frustrated thirteen-year-old tone, "Why can't you all understand? I only want to be an individual . . . just like everybody else!" *I only want to be an individual . . . just like everybody else.* I laughed as she stomped back to her room because that was the same paradox I was facing. On the one hand, I wanted to be courageous, to do something great and unique that I could be proud of. But on the other hand, I just wanted to blend in. I didn't want to do anything that might cause anyone to laugh at me or criticize me.

My sister is really no different than the rest of us. We want to be *different* somehow; we want to stand out, be noticed and be recognized. But on the other hand, we desperately want to feel accepted and be "just like everyone else." It's difficult to find that perfect balance between conformity and individuality, especially when you're dealing with the self-imposed restrictions of a comfort zone.

The desire to be different, however, can activate many of us. It can do so in two ways: one negative, the other positive. A negative desire to be different has little redeeming value because it is centered on three somewhat self-destructive concepts: (1) actions based on what others think of you, (2) actions based on comparisons to those around you, and (3) actions based on the desire to be *contrary* to the wish of authority figures. None of these three has ever really been the reason behind noteworthy success.

But a positive desire to be different—a desire that causes you to take a stand against evil or to try something new and creative that no one has attempted before—can move many individuals to achieve success. There's a difference between being *willing* to be different and just *choosing* to be different for the sake of being different. If you are willing to be different, then you most likely have a stronger, deep-rooted activating force behind your desire, such as the desire to be the (or *your)* best.

But the desire to be different, to be an "individual," is often so strong it can lead us to do stupid, even disastrous, things. For this reason, always look at the motives behind your desires to see if you're really on the right track toward wise decision-making. The following story is a disturbing example of why this is important.

An emergency room doctor tells the story of a teenage girl who had been in a serious car accident involving three other victims. All of them had been rushed to the hospital, but she was the only one conscious at the time. After she had been stabilized, this doctor tried to find out what had happened. The girl explained to the doctor that her parents had begged her not to go out with this particular boy she liked. According to them, he was disrespectful and not trustworthy, but all of her friends thought he was "cool." To let her parents know that she was old enough to make her own decisions, she had completely disregarded their tears and pleas and left the house. Soon the date had turned bad, and she was feeling quite uncomfortable with this boy, so she asked him several times to take her home.

Finally, in anger, he swung the car around and headed toward her house. Speeding and not driving responsibly, he approached a red light but never slowed down. They plowed into the side of a car passing through that intersection.

The girl then burst into tears and began telling the doctor how sorry she was for not listening to her parents, and then, realizing her need to speak with them, she asked the doctor if her parents were coming to the hospital to see her. Imagine the extreme difficulty for this doctor as he explained to this girl that the two passengers in the other car were her parents, and they had both been killed instantly.

This young girl decided to be different by rebelling. The risk she took was disastrous. But if your desire to be different comes from a desire to *make a difference,* the results can be impressive. There is a very productive side to being different, and it's the one that is generally more difficult to sustain—that is, being different in a positive, *good,* direction.

In *Discover* magazine, I read a fascinating article entitled "In the Earth but Not of It." The article reported, "The earth's inner core might as well be another planet. This 1,500-mile-wide sphere, made not of rock but of solid iron, is divided from the rest of the planet by the outer core—a moat of churning liquid iron, 1,300 miles thick. In 1996 it was reported that this planet-within-a-planet even spins at its own rate, outpacing the rest of Earth by about a quarter turn per century" (January 1997, 19). The article explains that the liquid iron in the "moat" is so hot that it's as thin as water, "so the inner core should be free to spin on its own, like a beach ball in a bathtub."

Hmm. Another planet. How many times has someone

said *you* are from another planet? That would be a sure sign you're a little, if not a lot, different. But are they saying it because you are following a tougher set of rules governed by an inner core of integrity? If so, then take it as a compliment. I think we would all love to be compared to "solid iron," different from the ordinary rock. To be made of solid iron is to be trusted, to be counted on not to change form when things get tough. Remember, "This planet within a planet even spins at its own rate, *outpacing the rest of Earth.*"

Yes, by choosing to live by concepts such as integrity and goodwill, you may often feel "out of step" with the rest of your peers, the community, or even with society in general. Remember, however, that while you might spin at your own rate, ultimately, just like the earth's inner core, you will "outpace" the rest of the world in the things that matter most. And that's a truly great and memorable way to be different.

## 5. THE DESIRE TO LET COURAGE, NOT FEAR, RUN YOUR LIFE

In the introduction to this book, I mentioned a critical decision I had made that affected nearly every other decision I have made the rest of my life: I decided I didn't want to be a coward in life. I wanted to be courageous! I wanted to be a rugged individualist, just like my great-great-grandpa Bunker. I made this decision when I was about fourteen years old; and because of it, I began a journey to find courage. I wasn't necessarily searching for the battlefield kind of courage and certainly not the triumph-over-tragedy kind of courage (I definitely didn't *want* any tragedy), but just the kind of courage that would push me into the room where auditions or interviews were being held. My desire to be courageous was just barely strong enough to override my fear of failure, which is precisely the reason I even dared to get on stage the first time the chance presented itself at age fourteen.

The choir director at school gave me an opportunity to test my courage. He walked into class one day and announced, "Hey, listen up everyone. I just got approval for us to put on a variety show for the whole school, and you don't even have to audition. Anyone can perform. Just let me know what you're going to do." I had always loved singing but had never been brave enough to sing by myself. My heart started racing just at the thought of being on stage by myself. I knew that trying a solo would be too much for my heart to handle, but maybe, just maybe, a duet would be okay. So I grabbed my best friend and begged her to sing a duet with me. And did we ever work hard on our song! We each had one verse to sing solo and then we came together in harmony for the chorus. My mom and dad told me I sounded great as I practiced.

The night of the performance came and, to be quite honest, I thought it went better than expected. I had been especially nervous my brain would freeze and I would forget the words or sing off-key. But I had remembered all the words and stayed on pitch, so I thought it was a hit. I had asked a friend to record our performance. When she gave me the cassette the next day, I rushed home to pop it in and listen for myself. As we all do when we hear ourselves on tape, I cringed at first. Then I listened carefully and, trying to be positive, I thought, "Well, I'm singing on pitch . . . and I remembered the words." Then I heard some laughter on the tape, while I was singing in the background. Apparently my friend had put her tape recorder on a table where a bunch of parents were sitting.

I heard the laughter and then I heard a woman say, "Oh, it's not that bad, is it?" Then there was more laughter, and the woman said, "Yeah, it's that bad!"

I was crushed. It's not too often that you get to hear on tape what people are saying behind your back. I felt completely worthless and humiliated. My parents had told me it was great! I went downstairs looking for my mom and told her what had happened. I was bawling. I said, "Mom, I'm never going to sing again, ever!" She listened and then said, "Oh, but you have a lovely voice, dear!" (We all know that's what a mom would say!) I told her I couldn't possibly ever sing again, especially not in front of people. We talked, and somehow she convinced me to at least keep singing in trios with my two younger sisters. She said, "No one will ever hear you in a trio." And I bought it. I decided I would continue to sing, but only with my sisters, or in choirs, or when I was all by myself at the piano.

After making this decision, I went on to make one of the biggest mistakes I could as I hovered between moving forward and jumping right back into my comfort zone. I did exactly what we all have a tendency to do. I kept replaying in my mind the laughter from those people I didn't even know, *instead of* replaying in my mind the words of support and encouragement from my family—those people I trust and admire and respect the most.

So for almost three years, I took my search for courage elsewhere. I tried out for the swim team. Nobody goes to watch swim meets—I'd be safe there. I tried out for the track team for the same reason, and it turned out to be fun. I sang in the chorus and even took up the trumpet so I could play in the band. (I primarily wanted to go on the fun trips our chorus and band went on every year!)

Then, just before my senior year, we moved to the

United States. A fresh start. On the one hand, it was kind of exciting to start swimming in a whole new pond, but on the other, it was like my comfort zone (which had begun to grow steadily) had shrunk back down. And it was then that my mom recognized her chance to once again help me do what I really loved to do. Mom suggested that I might want to take voice lessons to help build my confidence, and I thought it was worth a try. After a few months of lessons, I built up the courage to try out for the school's concert choir. And I made it . . . along with everyone else who tried out.

A few months later, when auditions were posted for the school musical, I knew I had progressed enough that I wouldn't embarrass myself, and maybe I'd even get a part. So I tried out because I didn't want to always wonder, *"What if?"* Well, the director didn't think much of me. I was the only senior who tried out who did not get a part. Instead, I was placed in the back with all the sophomores and juniors singing in the chorus. Nevertheless, my family and some friends still came to see me. I decided I needed to pay more attention to them and their encouragement. I felt more courageous around my encouragers. But right about the same time, I tried out for my favorite sport, volleyball, and didn't make the cut. So, I was left wondering if there was anything I was good at and what contribution I could possibly make to society. My guess is that most high school seniors graduate feeling pretty much the same.

The next year, I was a freshman at Brigham Young University. And despite everything that had happened in my past, I still liked to sing. I had a new voice teacher who, like my previous one, continually encouraged me. I never sang a solo, but I often sang with others . . . usually around the campfire or in church choirs. My sophomore year I continued with voice lessons. I was settling into my comfort zone quite nicely when my roommate, Robyn, came home one day and said, "Charlie (that's my nickname), you've got to go audition for Young Ambassadors!"

Young Ambassadors is an international performing group from BYU, specializing in high-energy dancing, singing, and musical theater. That year, about one thousand people tried out for this group, but only sixteen could make it. Many performers from the group have gone on to find successful careers on Broadway or in Nashville or elsewhere. So when Robyn suggested I try out, I laughed. I carefully explained to her my history of failure in the world of performing arts. Plus, I had never really danced before, another very important prerequisite for this group; trying out just didn't seem like a logical option for me. However, Robyn simply said, "What if you don't try out? Then you'll never know if you could have made it." Oh! She got me! I hate "what ifs." So even though I could still hear the laughter in the back of my mind, I realized that if I gave in to one fear, I would easily give in to others. I knew I needed to try out if for no other reason than to simply not give in to fear.

For the audition I had to prepare two songs. I walked into the small room, where two directors sat with a video recorder behind them. I began the first number; but after the first verse, the director cut me off and asked me to go on to the next one. *This is not a good sign,* I thought. I started singing my second song, where in the first few measures I had to drop from a high note to a very low note, at which time the director again interrupted me. "Was that an E flat below middle C?" he asked. (He obviously had perfect pitch). I said it was, and then he looked at his papers, lifted his head, and asked, "Why are you trying out as a soprano?" I responded, "Well, what do you need?" "We need altos," he stated. "I am an alto," I said in a distinctively lower voice. He looked down at his papers again then asked me if I had any dance experience, as he couldn't find anything listed on my sheet. "I've . . . well, I've been to a few," I said quietly.

I left the audition feeling embarrassed, but grateful that I wouldn't have to see any of the directors again. I was also proud of myself that I had not backed down from a scary thing. I *had* left my comfort zone, but I was now quite happy to head right back into that zone. I knew that my encouragers would still be encouraging even though I had obviously not performed well. I was pleased to note that my safety net was in place and holding.

The next day, Robyn asked if I had seen the callback list—because I was on it. "No way," I screamed. "Now what do I have to do?" "You have to dance," she responded. "Dance? I don't know how to dance!" It was then that I realized the time had come to once again venture outside my comfort zone.

I showed up to the dance audition wearing my usual jeans and sneakers. I walked into a huge hall where about five hundred people were warming up in leotards, jazz pants, and jazz shoes, with their legs stretched way up over their heads. I just stood there with my mouth open. Then a nice girl came over to me, startled me out of my stupor of thought, and suggested I take off my sneakers to dance. She offered me her extra pair of sweats to change into . . . along with a sleeveless, neon orange sweatshirt. After emerging from the dressing room and looking over the talented dancers before me, I felt like Rocky coming to work out with the cast from Fame.

The audition began with a very simple clapping routine,

and I thought, *This ain't so hard!* I guess they just wanted to see if we were somewhat coordinated. They called us up three at a time and I performed *okay,* but felt quite self-conscious the entire time. As soon as the music finished, I returned to my spot hugging the wall. I just knew the judges could tell I wasn't a dancer. But then the names of those who were invited to stay for the second round were announced, and mine was one of them! (I immediately thought, *Wow, I faked them out!* My motto ever since has been "Fake it 'til you make it!") Miraculously, I made it through two new rounds of tryouts, each more difficult than the first. (I think this was due to all the smiling and clapping I did. I just generally acted like I was having a good time, this seemed to make up for my lack of dance talent).

I then made it through more vigorous vocal auditions and eventually made it into Young Ambassadors. I asked my director a few months later how I ever got in (I didn't want to ask right away just in case he changed his mind). He said, "Well, we saw potential, and besides—we really needed a low alto!" Ugggh!

A low alto, huh? Ever since I had first started singing, I had been trying to be something that I thought people wanted. I thought they wanted *sopranos.* And so I kept trying to be a soprano. What a waste of energy. There I was, nearly twenty, and I had finally discovered I was an alto. It was that year—as an alto in the Young Ambassadors, traveling all over, performing, speaking, and, yes, even dancing—that I learned how to hold a microphone, how to speak and sing in front of an audience, how to feel comfortable on stage, and most especially, how to control my fears.

It was the very next year that I went back to Atlantic

City and, in front of a record television audience of more than 100 million people, won the Miss America title by playing the Paraguayan harp . . . and *singing*. I never in a million years would have won, had I not been in that performing group; and what if, *what if* my fear of failure had been stronger than my desire to be courageous, and I had stayed in a comfortable spot where I wouldn't get laughed at again? What if I had made a decision based on fear, not courage? I certainly would not have discovered that I'm an alto! I most definitely would have missed out on an incredible, singular experience as Miss America. Discoveries can only be made in uncharted territory . . . that territory outside your comfort zone.

Following my year as Miss America, I again had to decide just how far I wanted to leap out of my comfort zone. I went back to school for my junior year, which was surprisingly lonely and discouraging. I was criticized, ignored, hardly ever asked out on a date, and even then, was stood up four times . . . by four different guys. That certainly makes me normal though, doesn't it?

Even so, that wasn't the biggest step outside my comfort zone. About two weeks into that fall semester, the local CBS affiliate—KSL-TV—offered me a job and I told them that if I could do sports I might be interested. After my year-long experience with the press, I was no longer interested in broadcast journalism. But *sports*casting sounded fun.

Ever since I was a little girl I had preferred soccer balls to Barbie dolls. With a new network, ESPN, fulfilling every sports-lover's dream of twenty-four-hour sports programming, I realized there were a lot of opportunities for me to jump into the sporting news business. There was really only one credible woman on the air in those days—Gayle

Gardner with ESPN—but watching her made me think of how fun that would be. I wasn't necessarily a "sports nut," but I loved all kinds of competition as long as it was good. KSL-TV got back to me the next day and said, "We need a sideline reporter for the college football games we air. Will you do it?" Football? Well, never having actually seen the inside of a helmet, I wondered if this was just a bit too far out of my comfort zone. After all, I had to be realistic, didn't I? But then I reminded myself that I wanted to be courageous in life, not cowardly. So when presented with the opportunity to do something not exactly easy for me, I couldn't say no. Rugged individualists don't say no to opportunity.

During the next year I became a dedicated student of the game of football, learning much more than the average fan even wants to know. I spent several hours a week asking a lot of dumb questions to two very kind and patient BYU coaches—Dick Felt and Lance Reynolds. I watched "Monday Night Football" with friends who had played and constantly asked ridiculous questions. I also taped "Monday Night Football," then replayed anything I didn't understand.

At one of the first games I covered, I was allowed into the locker room for the few minutes of pep talk right before the game. It was my first time visiting the inner sanctum of college football. I stood in the corner of the main area, trying to be as inconspicuous as possible. All was quiet as the players focused on the game at hand. And then I heard the coach ranting and raving as he came down the hall. He stomped in, slammed a locker door, smacked a huge, three-hundred-pound lineman on the head, nearly knocking him over, kicked a garbage can across the room and then yelled: "This is war today, men! I want some casualties! Let 'em know you're out for blood, grind them into the ground! Make it so it *hurts* when they get up!" He paused for a moment and then said, in a much calmer voice, "Alright, let's pray." Is that all-American or what?

I prepared diligently for every game—hours and hours. I had a few people who encouraged me—like the head of the station, one of the coaches, the two men who were also part of the on-air team, and of course, my family. But on the whole I was roasted every week, mostly by people calling in to radio shows and saying, "Get that girl off the sideline!" Fans would yell things at me while I walked up and down the sidelines, and they would throw things at me too . . . like wet marshmallows (try getting one of those out of your hair! I began carrying little scissors around with me so I could cut out the marshmallows before I went on camera again. As the season progressed, my hair became shorter and shorter!). I would go home after games with zero self-esteem and think, *"Why am I taking such abuse? Why don't I go back to where I'm comfortable?"* But I stuck with it. And why? Shouldn't I have listened to all those guys who had played the game and didn't like me reporting on a game I had never played? I considered all that; but I had learned something about myself and I wasn't going to throw it away. I did have the courage not to be a coward. I wasn't going to back down and back away like I had when I was a kid. And besides, I had invested a lot of intellectual energy to understand the game, and I wasn't going to quit just when I was getting the hang of it.

Well, after three years, I thought that maybe I had gone just about as far as I wanted to go. Public flogging, which involved hearing jokes about me on the radio and being the subject of not-so-flattering editorial cartoons, was beginning to take its toll, and I was ready for the nice quiet life of an MBA student. But then ESPN saw my work and hired me. And you better believe it was one of the most thrilling moments of my life (upstaged only by my marriage and the births of our four children) to get that call from my agent, Michael Goldberg in New York City, telling me that ESPN—*ESPN*—wanted to sign me to a contract! And this was all at the time when I was beginning to think that maybe I had traveled that uncomfortable road full of criticism long enough. I didn't realize then that I still had more criticism to come! That's just the nature of being in the public eye. But at least my efforts to be courageous had paid off with a position on a national network.

What if I had listened more to the discouragers in my life and quit early on? What if I had thought that their opinions were more valid than my encouragers' cheers? I would have given up that very first season. I have often reflected on the incredible assignments I would have missed had I folded because I was just too uncomfortable.

Walking into ESPN headquarters in Bristol, Connecticut, was probably the biggest trip outside my comfort zone up until then. My boss showed me around SportsCenter, which is practically a men's locker room to me—although everyone walks around fully clothed, of course. I was introduced to Bob Ley, Chris Berman, and Charlie Steiner, and then my new boss sat me down in his office, looked me square in the eye, and started firing questions at me. "Who's leading the American League in RBIs?" "Name three of the top ten contenders for the Kentucky Derby." "What's the difference between the World Boxing Association and the International Boxing Federation?" All I could tell him was that I would go look it all up right away.

I immediately knew I had walked a mile out of my comfort zone, and this was one place I couldn't "Fake it 'til

I made it." I loved sports, loved competition, but I was not a walking sports trivia book, and I didn't even want to be. I also didn't want to give up. I didn't want to be a coward just when it got overwhelming and hard. So that afternoon I went out and bought every pack of bubble gum baseball cards I could find . . . and started memorizing the stats on the back of each card. I wondered what I had gotten myself into and, especially, if I could somehow convince my new colleagues that I could *learn*.

It took a while to feel comfortable there, but it happened when I stopped worrying about failure and the discouraging comments I received and instead focused on what I did *right* and *well*. I focused on anything and anyone encouraging. I soon found my niche, and it had nothing to do with being a walking trivia book. It had to do with my ability to learn fast, ask the right questions, empathize with my subject, and look comfortable and confident on TV.

The next time you are struggling to make a decision regarding which frog will most likely turn into royalty, try focusing on those positive forces that can help you choose a course of action: the desire to be happy, the desire to be the best, the desire to make a difference, the desire to *be* different, and above all, the desire to let courage run your life. Don't forget that, without a doubt, there will be many frogs that turn out to be nothing more than the homely creatures they have always been. At those times it will be tempting to give in to discouragement. So keep your positive forces right in the forefront of your thoughts and remember, we all have to kiss a lot of frogs before one will change dramatically right before our very eyes!

Chapter 6

# ELIMINATING THE DISCOURAGERS, FOCUSING ON THE ENCOURAGERS

By now, you probably recognize that you aren't the only person swimming around in your pond. Throughout your life you've let a number of people into your comfort zone—friends, parents, children, extended family, work associates, and so on. All of these people are at least somewhat interested in your success or failure. Many of them have probably helped you kiss a slimy frog or two.

Those individuals you have chosen to let into your comfort zone typically fit into one of two categories: those who encourage you and those who discourage you. The encouragers make you want to be a better person and make you feel like you *are* a better person. The discouragers tend to say things that make you feel like you are less of a person (these types of people also revel in the notion that the lower they make you feel, the better they are).

Identifying the people in your life who fit into each of these categories can help you to avoid the negative and deactivating effects that come from socializing with discouragers. It can also help you to surround yourself with people who will encourage you to take more chances, to do the hard things, to follow your dreams, and to leave your comfort zone more often. The better you are able to identify these people, the more control you will take over how much time you spend with them and how much influence you allow them to have over your thoughts.

Remember, however, that it's a slightly different story if you are a parent dealing with, shall we say, less than encouraging and positive children. It can be taxing on the mind and soul if you are constantly giving and building and serving children who not only seem completely oblivious to your efforts but who also seem to go out of their way to belittle you. My own children have not entered their teen years yet but have already developed some of the traditional teenage attitudes, as adorable as they are most of the time. Two years ago, when my second oldest daughter Nicole was six, I got a small inkling of what I might be in for down the road.

It was very early one morning when I heard some noise coming from the kitchen. I put on my robe and went to see which child was already up. There was Nicole up on the counter, reaching for the marshmallows (because, you know, that's what we eat every morning for breakfast), but before I could say anything, she took one look at my bed hair, my baggy eyes, my generally ragged appearance, and said, "Mom, if you were in the Miss America pageant today . . . you'd *lose*."

So much for thinking my children might treat me like Miss America.

One night I put dinner in front of my then-eight-year-old daughter, Monica, and she immediately wrinkled up her nose in distaste and proclaimed, "Ew, yuck!"

"But it's yummy, you'll like it!" I pleaded.

"Mom," she said in a surprisingly authoritative tone, "that's *opinion,* not fact."

I know these comments are mild—my children are still young—but even a six- and an eight-year-old can say things that are hurtful or make you doubt your abilities or general worth. When this happens—and you ladies who work the full-time job of mother and wife know this happens all the time—just consider the source, then get on the phone with a known encourager in your life and laugh about it.

## WHAT DRIVES YOU: CRITICISM OR APPROVAL?

There are different philosophies to coaching, training, and teaching. We have all seen them. Some believe in first tearing down their subjects in order to build them back up. Others use positive reinforcement as the primary tools for meeting their goals. Is one better than the other? In terms of teaching a skill, many feel that it all depends on the individual. But because every aspect of our life is interconnected, I believe that a positive and consistent approach throughout life, rather than a strong negative approach for smaller periods of time, has a greater overall effect on a person's abilities and capabilities. And yet, having said that, I acknowledge that there are many high-level athletes who are truly motivated to continue on even after their trusted mentors offer verbal attacks of every performance.

Many champions do, in fact, thrive on detailed and intense criticism of what they're doing. Other athletes, who aren't made of quite the same stuff, often buckle under such constant criticism. Certainly a world-class athlete must be able to withstand the intense pressure of world-class competition—and all the mind games that go with it—in order to perform at all. Sometimes those mind games are played with just the right mixture of light fun and serious purpose.

I met three-time world figure-skating champion Alexei Yagudin the day after he won the Olympic gold medal in spectacular fashion at the Salt Lake City 2002 Winter Games. I had always wanted to be part of the Olympics in one way or another, so when the Games came to Salt Lake, I volunteered for the most popular position available: a driver for one of the top Olympic sponsors. My particular assignment was to assist an executive with Visa International. Gold medalist Alexei was, of course, an in-demand celebrity, especially with the Olympic sponsors. And one day it just so happened that he and his agent/mentor Dimitri needed to ride in our car for a couple of Alexei's appearances with Visa.

None of us could resist asking him a few questions, and he graciously answered them all. When I asked him about dealing with the intense pressure of one billion people watching him for roughly four minutes, he laughed and said he never really thought about it. He just focused on his routine (which, by the way, included landing two quads and receiving an unprecedented four perfect 6.0s in presentation). Then Dimitri chimed in and told us the *real* reason Alexei hadn't thought about all those people. He said that Alexei was too focused on the things *Dimitri* had instructed him in the week before competition.

"I told him that if he didn't win, I would kill him," Dimitri said with a perfectly straight face and a thick Russian accent. When we all laughed, he added most seriously, "You think I'm joking? I was sharpening the knife all week long." It was obvious that this kind of "motivation" was a tool used to relieve tension while maintaining an understanding of significance between two adults who respected each other. I don't doubt that many more motivational words had been shared all week long (with a serious tone!). Dimitri's penchant for humor made him just the right kind of encourager for Alexei, who will most likely go down as one of skating's all-time greats.

It is often up to the coach to discover how much his or her athlete can take, and what "buttons" to push to achieve the desired results. Some athletes need a tiger swiping at them to push the adrenaline and the desire even higher. Some athletes need an intellectual, strategic, and calm approach and are not moved by motivational theatrics. One coach who knows how to identify these different kinds of buttons is Pat Summitt, head coach of the University of Tennessee Lady Vols and winner of five NCAA championships. In her book, *Reach for the Summit* (a book I like to use as my parenting handbook, by the way), Coach Summitt explains how she is able to find exactly what motivates each individual player on her team. She uses a survey called the "Predictive Index" to categorize personality traits—some people are authoritative, some are craftsmanlike, some are methodical, and so on. Here are a few of her thoughts:

"When I look at the personality profile of a player, it doesn't matter what his or her physical body type is. I'm more concerned with the mind attached to it. If I understand the inner workings of someone, I know better how to motivate him or her" (New York: Broadway Books, 1998, 144).

"I do believe that there is a basic blueprint for coaxing performances out of athletes or any other talented people. The blueprint is this: knowledge, confidence, relaxation, results. Knowledge builds confidence, which causes you to be relaxed, which gives you good results. . . .

"The more I know our players, the better we will be able to duplicate the circumstances that are conducive to their best performances. I'll give you an example. The Predictive Index describes Type D people as perfectionists. They walk around in a flinch mode, waiting for something bad to happen. They think about what will happen not if but when they make a mistake. So when I pull a player like that from a game, I don't yell at her. I ask her, 'What did you do wrong?' She tends to already know the answer. My response is, 'That's right. Now, I want you to have a rest, because I'm going to put you back in the game in a few minutes.' If I don't reassure that person, she'll sit on the bench and play the game over again mentally. When she goes back in, she'll still be thinking about the mistake she made before. I don't want her thinking about the mistake she made before, I want her to play the game front-ward, not backward" (ibid., 145).

"The personality profile gives me a tool when I need a way to reach a player. If all her life she's thrived on approval, then I use that to motivate her. I hunt for ways to draw her best out. To be honest, I push her buttons" (ibid., 147).

I would have thrived on Coach Summitt's team because I thrive on approval, not put-downs. I have to admit that I'm one of those people who takes criticism personally—even if it has to do with a skill I know I should separate from who I am as a person. Because of this, I have learned to mentally discount the "discouraging words" I hear and try hard to focus on the encouraging ones until I discover for myself that I can be confident in the task at hand and truly enjoy it. I have promised myself that, despite discouragers, I will stay with something if (1) I don't want to stop trying because I like it or (2) I have made a commitment and will therefore see it through. Sometimes, though, I do choose another path and give something up, but only after a lot of thought and some good self-analysis. So why do *you* choose to quit . . . or proceed?

## WHAT TO DO WITH THE NEGATIVE WORDS WE HEAR FROM OTHERS

One of the most helpful tools in determining whether you want to proceed with an endeavor or exercise a different talent elsewhere is the words you hear from others. And some of us listen more carefully to what those around us are saying than others. (If a *dream* is involved, however, the situation becomes a little bit different because dreams tend to override negative comments coming from any direction.) In my life, I have discovered that discouraging words *de*activate me. They make me go elsewhere. Why would I want to hang around anyone who makes me feel down on myself? Even if the person's ulterior motive is to make me excel, I feel that there are better ways to help me achieve greatness than through humiliation. Encouraging people, however, *act*ivate me. They show me the stars, give me hopes and dreams, and make me feel like I can do *anything*. Who wouldn't want to be around such motivation?

Right after I won Miss Utah (a competition I entered because my mom said she thought I could do it), I was told I had to be "coached" to prepare for the Miss America pageant that September. After my first "mock" interview, I felt demoralized. It didn't go well at all. I certainly wasn't prepared to hear criticism. I was looking for advice. I left the session feeling like I stood no chance at all of winning the Miss America title. I went home that evening and told my parents I would have fun and certainly do my best at the pageant, but I couldn't even hope to win. I felt that the "experts" had placed me far below the standard for winning in every category. My parents knew immediately that I had been in the presence of "discouragers" all day.

We talked it over and decided that I had to give myself the best chance at winning . . . and that meant pulling myself away from anyone discouraging in my life. So instead of following a prescribed preparation routine that included a host of mock interviews, I spent a lot of time discussing issues with my encouragers, who were mostly family members and friends. I talked things over and voiced my opinions freely instead of participating in what I felt were stale question-and-answer scenarios. The mock interviews I had been in before only made me more hesitant to say what I really thought, not less. I knew myself well enough to know that too much criticism during my preparation would cause me to clam up.

I also listened to talk radio a lot, and often I would turn down the volume and pretend I was a caller voicing my opinion on the issue being discussed. Just the thought of actually being on the air gave me the same adrenaline rush I knew I might experience as I walked into a room full of judges. The more I practiced my "radio call-ins" (and you can imagine all the strange looks I got from passengers in other cars), the easier it became to verbalize my thoughts. I would give myself 45 seconds to answer a question, then 30 seconds, and then just 15. I visualized doing everything right, and carefully listened to my encouragers when they offered suggestions.

I had to go with my gut feeling on this, even though

most people thought I was crazy for not following the pre-scribed routine of these things. I also recognized that *con-structive* criticism was an integral part of my preparation, so I asked those people I trusted and respected most (once again, my "encouragers") for all the constructive criticism they could offer. For me to accept criticism, I have to respect the deliverer of the bad news. It was more impor-tant to me to head back to Atlantic City with my encour-agers solidly backing me—ready to catch me should I fall miserably—than to be dependent on discouragers, whom I felt would disown me in failure, claiming they had nothing to do with how I turned out anyway. It was a thrilling experience to look over at my small group of "encouragers" lining the wall at my first press conference as Miss America.

## FOCUSING ON THE ENCOURAGERS

In 1989, as a young reporter with ESPN, I was assigned to cover stellar high school athletes for a weekly program called "Scholastic Sports America." One highlighted athlete was a fifteen-year-old girl who had been a professional tennis player for only a few months and yet was zooming upward through the rankings. I was fascinated by this very talented, endearing, and intelligent (she was a straight-A student, and English was her second language!) teenager. Interestingly though, her professional beginnings were rocky and somewhat discouraging, not because she didn't have the talent, but because she did things a little differ-ently than most. Consequently, she had been openly criti-cized. Because her technique was unlike anything her peers had ever dealt with before, many called her style ridiculous.

Her backhand was common enough (a powerful two-handed stroke), but her forehand . . . well, she used two hands on that stroke as well. That was practically unheard of! It seemed awkward, too off-balance, and her peers told her it would never withstand the rigorous exchanges among the world's best. And something else made them laugh as well. Every time she hit the ball, a loud, resonating grunt escaped from her, punctuating the force she directed toward the other side of the net. She was constantly teased by opponents, by the media, and by the fans. At one prestigious tournament, one opponent publicly humiliated her by refusing to even play her unless she stopped grunting, claiming that it was simply too distracting.

Her father had taught her this technique, explaining to us that she was able to get more power into her swing by expelling the air from her lungs rapidly when she hit the ball and as her arms came across her chest—in much the same way a weightlifter gets a bit more ability to push the weight upward. Anytime air is exhaled so forcefully, there will be a loud noise. So, at this tournament, she briefly tried to keep quiet, but it hurt her game. Despite the critics, she stuck with her unusual double-handed forehand and the grunting. She made the courageous decision to tune out the "discouragers" and listen to her true "encouragers." She understood that this technique was in fact part of why she was able to win, and to cave in to the jeers would really just hurt her in the long run.

Two years after turning pro, the laughing stopped. Why? Because Monica Seles became the youngest tennis player ever to turn number one in the world. Young women all over the world started grabbing their rackets with both hands, and tennis fans everywhere began hearing a lot more noise coming from the up-and-coming, more forceful players. She stood alone and dared to try something new, even in the face of prospective failure and criticism. And that's what made her a champion. The same day Monica became number one, my first child was born. Remembering the unique individual I had spent two days getting to know a few years before, we named our daughter Monica. In 1999, I watched Monica Seles play in the U.S. Open semifinals against Serena Williams and had to chuckle at what I saw and *heard*. Monica wasn't the only one with a "grunt" to write about—Serena matched her grunt for grunt . . . and then went on to win the U.S. Open. It looks like the grunting is here to stay.

Being around encouraging people, or even just one encouraging person, can literally make the difference between being brave enough to give it a shot . . . or not. It can be the difference between ultimate success and failure. I dared to try out for that performing group because of one encouraging comment from my roommate—and a few additional ones from my mom and dad when they learned what I was up to. Monica Seles dared to stick with her ridiculed technique because of one encourager, her father. And naturally, the most important encourager really boils down to you, just you. If you can't accept encouragement—choosing instead to dismiss it as non-substantive or "biased" (like I sometimes did)—then a crucial part of your safety net is missing. It's just that much harder to feel comfortable outside your comfort zone. So even if you are incredulous and can think of a bunch of reasons why you shouldn't believe them, lean on your encouragers anyway. Quite often, others can see something in you that you've altogether missed.

One of my favorite stories of encouragement is the "story-behind-the-story" of one of the greatest works of music ever composed. It is the story of Sergei Rachmaninoff, born in Novgorod, Russia, April 1, 1873. He was brought up in an aristocratic, musically talented family. Young Sergei excelled in music. At age nine, he was enrolled in the St. Petersburg Conservatory and was later awarded the Great Gold Medal for excellence in composition and performance from the Moscow Conservatory. In 1897, at age twenty-three, he premiered his much-anticipated first symphony, the *Symphony No. 1 in D Minor,* played by the Russian Symphony Society. For Sergei it was a disaster, in great part due to the drunken condition of the conductor and his poor performance. The reviews were exceptionally harsh. One well-respected critic, Cesar Cui, scathingly remarked in the newspapers the next day that Rachmaninoff would surely win first place for his symphony "if there was a conservatory in Hell."

"If there was a conservatory in Hell," he wrote, "and if one of the talented pupils there was commissioned to compose a symphony based on the story of the 'Seven Egyptian Executions,' and if he composed one resembling that of Rachmaninoff's, he would have brilliantly accomplished his task and would have brought ecstasy to the inhabitants of Hell" (Cesar Cui in Victor Seroff, *Rachmaninoff* [N.Y.: Simon and Schuster, 1950], 62).

Cui also called Rachmaninoff's symphony "diseased" with "perverted harmonizations that created a morbid atmosphere" (ibid.).

Ironically, this was the work that, following Rachmaninoff's death, was acclaimed by many musicologists as his greatest contribution to symphonic literature as well as his most original composition. At the time, however, Rachmaninoff could not see into the future. He only saw the present and the humiliating failure that had befallen him. He wrote: "Something within me snapped.

All my self-confidence broke down. A paralyzing apathy possessed me. I did nothing at all and found no pleasure in anything. Half my days were spent on a couch sighing over my ruined life. My only occupation consisted in giving a few piano lessons to keep myself alive" (in Utah Symphony Program Notes, 27–28 February 1998, 20).

Indeed, Rachmaninoff stopped composing altogether and turned to conducting and performing other composers' music. But given that his true love was in composition, he fell into a state of depression that nearly ended his career. For three years he languished. His "comfort zone" continued to shrink until finally, in 1900, his concerned friends and family begged him to seek psychiatric help from Dr. Nikolai Dahl, a sophisticated music-lover and talented amateur violinist. Dr. Dahl performed a miracle with the simple power of *encouraging* suggestions. Rachmaninoff later described how he was transformed and released from his depression:

"My relations had told Dr. Dahl that he must at all costs cure me of my apathetic condition and achieve such results that I would again begin to compose. Dahl had asked what kind of composition they wanted and had received the answer, 'A concerto for piano,' for this is what I had promised to the people in London, and I had given it up in despair. Consequently, I heard the same hypnotic formula repeated day after day while I lay half asleep in an armchair in Dahl's study. 'You will begin to write your concerto. . . . You will write with great ease. . . . The concerto will be a fine work. . . .' It was always the same, without interruption. Although it may sound incredible, this cure really worked. At the start of the summer I began to compose again. The material grew in bulk, and new musical ideas began to stir within me—far more than I needed for my concerto. By the autumn I had finished two movements of the concerto—the Andante and the Finale. I played the two movements during that autumn at a charity concert. They had a gratifying success. This buoyed up my self-confidence so much that I began to compose again. By the spring I had already finished the first movement of the concerto and the suite for two pianofortes. I felt that Dr. Dahl's treatment had strengthened my nervous system to a miraculous degree. Out of gratitude, I dedicated my Second Concerto to him" (ibid.).

The Concerto had its first complete performance at a Philharmonic Society concert in Moscow on November 9, 1901, with the composer as soloist. If you haven't already heard the floating, lyrical passages all throughout Rachmaninoff's Concerto No. 2, go find it and see if you don't agree with me that its melodies are truly unsurpassed. As a senior in high school, there was nothing I wanted to play more than that piano concerto. Though I never really perfected it, I did learn at least the first movement. That was one—and perhaps the *only*—piece of music I never got tired of practicing. It moved me every time, and still does. And to think Rachmaninoff might have never found the courage to write it!

Rachmaninoff was extremely productive in the sixteen years following his triumph over depression. He composed more than fifty piano works, two piano sonatas, his third concerto, his second symphony, *The Isle of the Dead,* two operas, and various other works. In 1917, the Russian Revolution forced him to leave Russia when he lost his home. In the United States he became a concert pianist, and toward the end of his career he began composing again. He then completed the *Paganini Rhapsody* (see the movie *Somewhere in Time,* starring Christopher Reeve and

Jane Seymour, if you want to hear it accompany a good story!) and his third symphony. Again, he was harshly criticized. But this time he had learned how to deal with his critics. He had built the courage he needed to defend himself and ignored them by saying, "Personally, I'm firmly convinced that this is a good work. But, sometimes the author is wrong too! However, I maintain my opinion" (ibid.).

I am continually amazed by the power of positive, encouraging suggestions. It certainly doesn't have to take place in a doctor's office to be just as effective. I heard continual encouraging comments from my parents, grandparents, siblings, true friends, and good teachers.

One of the best things I've ever done is to keep in touch—even if just once a year during the holidays—with those who have encouraged me throughout my life. One of the other best things I've ever done is to throw away the addresses and phone numbers of all those who made it a point to discourage me.

## WHO ARE YOUR ENCOURAGERS?

As you contemplate who the encouragers in your life are, don't forget to consider how much you trust them and why you trust them. Those you can trust will always have your best interests at heart.

And remember, at the same time you embrace the encouragers, dismiss, disregard, and disconnect the discouragers from your lives. If the discouragers are part of your own family or work associates, then you probably won't be able to get rid of them completely. And I wouldn't recommend doing so, either. Instead, connect a voice-messaging system into that part of your brain that handles incoming messages. Leave instructions that discouraging messages are not to be forwarded to the rest of your brain. Encouraging messages, however, are allowed unlimited access.

Embrace the encouragers and dismiss the discouragers. That's the best way to begin creating a safety net that you can use as you venture out to find those frogs.

Chapter 7

# DECIDING WHAT YOU'RE REALLY AFTER

Now that kissing a frog doesn't seem too impossible, you need to decide what you want to get out of your risky endeavor. Where do you want to end up? At the top? Somewhere in the middle? And doing or achieving what? Do you want to stay outside your comfort zone for a long time or only for short periods of time? If you have trouble identifying the "who" and the "what" that drive you to make a decision, then focus on the "where." It's just like algebra—by figuring out one side of the equation, you'll figure out the other.

Let's assume that you are like most people and you want to be better and do better. Having established that, ask yourself a few questions: Where, exactly, is *better*? Are you happy with your destination being anywhere but down? Or do you want to make it to the very top? As you consider the possibilities, don't forget to include in the equation your "encouragers" and the *act*ivating forces that motivate you. These are, after all, half of your "safety net" and they make it easier to be comfortable outside your comfort zone.

## THE WATCH

I recently read a fascinating account of one person who was unbelievably focused and absolutely sure of exactly what he wanted. His story is found in the *New York Times* best-selling book *Seabiscuit: An American Legend,* about one of the most famous thoroughbreds in history. Because I have covered the Kentucky Derby and the Preakness for almost a decade, I have developed a special interest in thoroughbred racing. Author Laura Hillenbrand's book is a remarkable look at Seabiscuit, his great feats, and all aspects of the thoroughbred industry, including the injury-ridden world of jockeys. Of the latter, Hillenbrand writes:

"Nothing tops the strange fate of Ralph Neves, a hot-headed, hardriding teenaged jockey known as 'the Portuguese Pepperpot.' In the spring of 1936 Bing Crosby offered a $500 watch to the jockey who won the most races at California's Bay Meadows Racecourse. By the penultimate day of the meet, Neves was two wins in front of his nearest competitor and riding with a fury. That afternoon, rolling around the far turn aboard a horse named Flanakins, Neves was in the lead and looking like a cinch to win Crosby's prize. But without warning, Flanakins stumbled and crashed, catapulting Neves into the rail. Flipping to the track, Neves was trampled by trailing horses. Flanakins rose, uninjured—Neves had broken her fall—but the jockey lay motionless. Two physicians in the crowd sprinted out to him, joining the track doctor. They declared Neves dead on the track. The race caller made the somber announcement and asked the crowd to stand in prayer. As the sickened spectators bent their heads and reporters rushed to get word to their editors, Neves's body was carried to a mortuary. His toe was tagged, and he was parked on a table to await funeral arrangements.

"Physician Horace Stevens, a friend of Neves's, got word of his death and went to view the body. When he arrived, Stevens noticed something the track doctors had missed. He prepared a syringe and injected Neves with adrenaline.

"Neves woke up.

"A few minutes later, he stumbled out of the mortuary and onto the street, where he caught a cab, sped back to Bay Meadows, jumped out and began rushing toward the jockeys' room. As the shirtless, blood-splattered erstwhile corpse sprinted past the grandstand, astonished fans started running after him. By the time Neves hit the wire, most of the crowd was chasing him. He shook loose from the mob, dashed past the clubhouse, and burst into the jockeys' room, a boot on one foot and, apparently, a toe tag on the other. He scared the bejesus out of everyone.

"When the jockeys recovered from the shock, they took Neves, kicking and screaming, down to the first-aid room. He insisted that he was going to ride the rest of the card. The incredulous stewards refused. Neves went home, still fixated on that watch. He came back the next day loaded for bear. While San Franciscans were reading his obituary in several papers, the decidedly undead Neves rode like a man possessed and won the watch. Reports of his death were fifty-nine years premature" (New York: Ballantine Books, 2001, 75–76).

## WHAT EXACTLY DO YOU WANT?

You may not be fixated on a watch like Ralph Neves, but it helps to be fixated on something. What is it you want? What is the reason you get up in the morning and do anything during the day? What is your purpose? What do you hope to accomplish? Popularity? Fortune? Are you sure? I once read a small paragraph in *Parade* magazine in response to a question regarding who attended the funeral of film legend Ava Gardner. This was the sad answer: "Though Ava Gardner was world famous for her sultry beauty, 60 films, three husbands (Mickey Rooney, Artie Shaw, and Frank Sinatra) and numerous lovers (including Robert Taylor and George C. Scott), she spent her final years as a recluse in a London apartment. Her only companions were her longtime housekeeper, Carmen Vargas, and beloved Welsh corgi, Morgan. Sinatra reportedly paid her medical expenses after a 1986 stroke left Gardner partially paralyzed and bedridden. After the actress died of pneumonia in 1990 at 67, Vargas took her body home to her native North Carolina for a private burial. None of Gardner's ex-husbands attended" (Walter Scott's Personality Parade, 12 March 2000).

She was considered one of the most beautiful movie stars ever, but died alone with no family or wealth to speak of. I wonder if all her film accomplishments and popularity back in the heyday of Hollywood brought her any comfort. Think carefully about what you want.

One of my favorite books is *Hope for the Flowers* by Trina Paulus (New York: Newman Press, 1972), in which the author tells the story of Stripe, a hungry young caterpillar.

Stripe joins a large number of squirming, pushing caterpillars, each of which is struggling to climb a great column that rises into the air and disappears into the clouds. Stripe sees that the caterpillars are all intent on trying to reach the top of the column, but since its top is obscured by the clouds, he has no idea what he might find there. Even so, Stripe pushes upward with his fellows.

The journey is not easy. Stripe is pushed and kicked

and stepped on from every direction. Climb or be stepped on seems to be everyone's motto.

Full of agitation, Stripe asks a fellow crawler, "Do you know what's happening?"

"'I just arrived myself,' said the other. 'Nobody has time to explain; they're so busy trying to get wherever they're going up there.'

"'But what's at the top?' continued Stripe.

"'No one knows that either, but it must be awfully good because everybody's rushing there. Goodbye; I've got no more time!'"

The story goes on at some length. The thing Stripe learns is that his mindless struggle to climb over others and get to the top is a futile, pointless endeavor. His ambition costs him for a time the things that would be of true worth to him—companionship and love—and it is not until he gives up his empty quest that he reaches his full potential and becomes a beautiful butterfly, capable of flying to the top.

## BE SPECIFIC: HAVE A GOOD PLAN

What are worthy goals to you? How do you really define success? Not only is it a useful exercise to write down some goals you would like to aim for—the reasonable as well as the seemingly "unreasonable" or "unattainable" ones—but it is also important to write down next to each one the *reason* you are pursuing these things. *Why* do you want to be recognized by your peers? *Why* do you want to become a millionaire? What is the driving force behind your ambitions? There are *dreams*, and then there are *priorities*. Sometimes the two are compatible, but what if they aren't?

In this search for what you think is worth leaving your

comfort zone, consider the importance of a logical and rational approach to how far and how high you might be reaching. If the reach is completely unreasonable—let's say you enter a triathlon though you have only previously competed in a 5k and you have never trained for biking and swimming—then the likelihood of coming in first is an extreme long shot. But once the training has taken place, the reach is no longer unreasonable. Should perfection be part of your goal? No, it shouldn't. But *progression* is something you should continually strive for. As one author puts it, "the quest for the best has serious side effects and may be causing more problems than successes. There is evidence that it may not be worth it to be perfect—at least not all of the time.

"Simply put, a perfectionist is someone whose achievement level has gone awry. He or she strains compulsively toward improbable goals, basing self-worth on achievements. As a result, errors and mistakes terrorize them. When they do succeed, it is not enough. They must do better. They are driven, but unable to really enjoy their accomplishments" (Perry W. Buffington, "Perfection: Impossible Dream?" *Sky,* August 1987).

Value the process of progressing as you keep pushing those comfort zone boundaries outward. As you make plans and set goals, there will be inevitable setbacks that make you wonder if there's a point to making a plan at all. Why not just wait and see what opportunities knock you down? I wouldn't be a true sportscaster if I didn't quote Vince Lombardi at least once: "You don't win once in a while. You don't win by accident. Winning is a habit, just like losing. You must plan if you're to be a winner."

And be specific about goals. Winners are always specific and positive, but losers tend to be general and negative.

There's a classic exchange in Lewis Carroll's *Alice in Wonderland* that depicts the senseless meandering that comes from having no specific plan:

Alice: Would you tell me please which way I ought to go from here?

Cat: That depends a good deal on where you want to get to.

Alice: I don't much care where—

Cat: Then it doesn't matter which way you go.

Alice: . . . so long as I get *somewhere*.

Cat: Oh you're sure to do that, if you only walk long enough (Mt. Vernon, N.Y.: The Peter Pauper Press, 1866, 79).

Although behaving like Alice in some things will get you nowhere, it is okay to take up one of her habits for a few minutes. Daydream. Think about what's really worth getting uncomfortable about—finding a job you're really happy in? Improving your marriage even though you might have to take the first step? Becoming a better, more persuasive speaker? Getting physically fit?

Go ahead and write down your goals. Just because they are written down does not mean you are a "failure" if they are not achieved right away. As long as you are continually searching for the right frog, then your comfort zone will grow; and that dynamic activity constitutes success and satisfaction in and of itself. Remember to be specific about what frog you are looking for, and it will make your search much easier. Then identify the motives underlying that specified goal to confirm that you do, in fact, really want the royal life.

## Step 3

# WORK WITH THE TOOLS THAT WILL HELP YOU DO THE HARD THINGS

### Getting the Guts
### to Approach the Frog

Chapter 8

# ESTABLISHING ABSOLUTES IN A WORLD OF CHANGE

Everyone has heard the worn-out saying that the only absolutes in life are death and taxes. Yet as trite as the phrase has become, it *really doesn't seem possible* that we can count on anything . . . other than death and taxes. There are, in fact, few people most of us can count on at all times and in all situations; and there certainly are not any future plans we can count on. Based on all of this not-so-encouraging information, can you think of anything that is absolute? Let's say you do get the courage to kiss a frog, and he does turn into a handsome prince, how can you guarantee he won't change back into a slimy amphibian over the course of time? Is there anything so sure and so solid that you can stake your life on the fact that it will never change? Many people will tell you, no way. But I will boldly say, yes, there is.

I not only challenge the belief that there are no absolutes in life, I firmly assert the opposite. There *are* absolutes in life; and the more resolute you are in those absolutes, the more courage you own to do the hard things that crop up in life. Courage is born of fundamental principles and priorities, not ambivalence or indifference. Can you imagine someone finding the courage to put his or her very life on the line for a casual interest in something? I doubt it. You find courage when you really believe in something. The more you have to believe in, the more courage you have.

So, to have courage you must create an "absolute" foundation in your life that doesn't shift and doesn't tumble when the forces of nature or mankind create chaos. If you discover, to your dismay, that you have no foundation, then build one. Dismiss the excuses, and just build one. Decide and confirm what absolutes you want to be made of. This isn't time-consuming and it isn't hard. You just have to think about it for a little while. This chapter will help you get started.

## UNCOVERING PERSONAL ABSOLUTES

I define *absolutes* as anything of significance that doesn't change, regardless of all the change or chaos going on around and/or within an individual. I uncovered my personal absolutes as a naïve twenty year old suddenly thrown into a strange and chaotic, albeit exciting, world of fleeting fame and some measure of fortune. It was the year I became Miss America.

I entered the Miss America program on a lark—based mostly on my mom's encouragement and the desire for a cash scholarship. After winning the Miss Utah pageant, I headed for Atlantic City during the most turbulent time in the program's history. For the first time ever, a reigning Miss America had been forced to resign about two months prior because of pictures that had been published of her in *Penthouse* magazine. This was a controversial action that sparked quite a few debates nationwide.

Some decried her resignation, saying the program was antiquated and she should be allowed to do whatever she wanted, like all other women her age. They said that moral issues had no place in the "real world." Others countered by saying that moral issues not only have a place in today's world but should also be more central to our society. They said that Miss America was not just another scholarship program but an opportunity to be a role model. None of us really knew what the judges would be looking for in this climate . . . a "woman of the world" or a nun? I assumed they would probably be more interested in a cosmopolitan, sophisticated woman of the 1980s and not what they might perceive to be an anachronistic pioneer woman from Utah.

When I arrived, I instantly felt as though I had landed in a foreign country. The glitz and glamour were strange for this tomboy who lived in jeans and sneakers. I took it all in with a combination of awe and amusement, as well as a measure of inadequacy. The first day at the pageant was eerily similar to the first day of junior high. It seemed like everyone else knew what to do, where to go, and what to *wear*. Because of the scandal, between four hundred and five hundred members of the press from all over the world—England, France, Japan, Canada, Australia, Germany, Argentina, and more—were in attendance. It was tabloid heaven. There was more interest in this program than ever before.

In the first few minutes after the initial orientation, we were asked to stand in alphabetical order so the press could easily find us. Soon, I noticed that several members of the press were approaching me. I was excited about the possibility of being noticed, so I stood a little straighter and smiled at them as they asked, "Miss Utah? Could you step aside? We need to get a picture of Miss Texas." I moved over (graciously, I hope) and decided I had better be realistic about the whole thing. Why would anyone notice me anyway?

Because things had not gone well with the press, I had no expectations that it would be better with the judges. Nonetheless, I did my best and soon found myself in the top ten on the final night of competition. The ten of us were reduced in number to six, from which the new Miss America would be crowned (way back then they didn't go down to the last two finalists in order to create suspense). The emcee, Gary Collins, then announced, "The new Miss America is Miss Utah, Sharlene Wells!" My first thought was, *My brothers are not going to believe this!* After the walk down the runway and the usual hugs and tears, a pageant official took me to a small room where she asked if I was ready for my press conference. Press conference? Nobody had wanted to talk to me before, so I was somewhat dumbfounded at the thought of facing the press corps now. But the doubt went away quickly, and I thought, *Sure, I'm ready. This should take only about five minutes.* I nodded that I was ready.

The pageant official opened two big double doors and escorted me into a large hall filled with reporters from all over the world. As I walked in, there was immediate chaos. Suddenly the reporters started yelling questions while flashes went off and television cameras began filming. I immediately felt fear.

A thousand thoughts ran through my head. Before that evening's competition, I had convinced myself that they didn't like me, so why would they like me now? Would they approve of me? Would they criticize me? Finally, my mind cleared. Then I did one of the smartest things I've ever taken credit for. I thought of the things that really mattered most to me in life—my "absolutes," those things that absolutely do not change regardless of all the change around me—and I knew that I didn't care what the press thought. I really didn't. I cared what *I* thought, what God thought, and what my encouragers thought of me. I realized I had a safety net, one that would allow me to explore any great heights or any wide abyss without fear of complete destruction. These things gave me courage and confidence to "boldly go" where I had never gone before. I was suddenly very aware that my life could change drastically from everything that I was accustomed to—for good and bad.

## FORTIFYING YOUR ABSOLUTES

At different periods of life, each of us experiences change. It may come in the form of a relationship that is ending or one that is just beginning. It may come with the news that someone you love has been diagnosed with a life-threatening disease. It may be a lost job or your first day at a new one. It may be your first day back at school or your last child's first day of kindergarten. Any change is scary, very simply because the *unknown* is scary. But if you have structure amidst change, you will have confidence to adapt—and that's when you get comfortable outside your comfort zone! *Your absolutes are that structure.* Build the structure, fortify it, be secure in it, and nothing will knock it down, no matter what unknowns you step into. We all need something strong in our lives to give us peace and purpose. Absolutes don't just float away with the tide.

I'd like to share five of my absolutes (I thought consciously of only the first three at my first Miss America press conference, but I have a bunch more), and as I do, I invite you to think about yours.

## MY ABSOLUTES

- I put my trust in God. (Every coin in America supports me in this.)
- I define real success and happiness by my relationships, not my accomplishments or financial success.
- My opinion of myself does not rest in the hands of others. I decide it.
- I always aim for big dreams and excellence. That means I must leave my comfort zone and be more courageous than cowardly.
- I never allow failure to defeat me. I do, however, reserve the right to change direction if common sense and respected individuals assist me in the decision to change course. But I don't give up because it gets hard. *Defeat the defeat,* I always say.

As I embarked on a year of service as Miss America, I discovered that the stronger my absolutes were, the stronger my courage became! I slowly developed into the rugged individualist I wanted to be, knowing I could handle more and more with each new step outside my comfort zone. If I had had no absolutes, I would have been nothing more than a chameleon—the adorable little lizard that changes colors depending on the environment he's in.

## TESTING MY ABSOLUTES

Now, let me get back to my story.

With all those reporters yelling at me, but having just thought of my absolutes, I felt an immediate surge of courage and confidence, peace and purpose. I walked over to the podium, asked everyone to sit down, and said, "Be quiet, raise your hands, and I'll call on you one at a time!" And they did! I pointed to one man and said sweetly, "Reporter from Texas? Could you please move? I'd like to speak with the reporter from Utah right behind you." Okay, I really didn't do that. At first I was asked superficial questions: What's your favorite vegetable? Do you have a boyfriend? And then the questions became more intriguing: What's your view on abortion? Your view on ERA?

Then one reporter asked me how this was going to change my life. I knew he was probably thinking of the limousines I would now be using, the first-class plane seats, the fancy clothes, the trips to the White House, and so on. I was never more focused than when I answered him directly and said, "It's not going to change my life. The things that matter most to me now will always matter the most to me. I'll learn a lot, experience a lot, but it won't change who I am."

I traveled a quarter of a million miles that year—five cities a week. My absolutes were tested over and over again. I had to get used to it right from the start; reporters all over the world joked about my conservative values and called me old-fashioned. Cartoonists and comedians had material for new jokes. Even Bob Hope, who aired his yearly special just a few days after I won, opened his show with jokes about me. I thought this one was especially funny: "So the new Miss America is from Utah. Well, did you know she is so conservative that she couldn't use the swimsuit she brought with her because it had a hole . . . in the *knee?*" Hah, hah.

At first I was embarrassed, but then I thought, *You*

*know, I could have done something a lot worse than just being a goody-goody.* So I got used to it. But I never got used to being halfway across the country, casually reading a newspaper in someplace I had never been before and suddenly seeing my name pop up. Like when one reporter wrote about Bob Guccione and his *Penthouse* magazine. The reporter suggested that "Sharlene Wells should give [Guccione] a call and demand that he change the name to *Re*penthouse!" I thought it was actually a clever idea.

A year as Miss America is a hard one for anyone who carries the title (yes, I can just see everyone pulling out their tiny violins). In fact, most Miss Americas go through some kind of a depression simply because they are not at all accustomed to the constant criticism. No one likes criticism—especially when it's public. I am often asked what that year was like and I have finally figured it out. It was sort of like going into a grocery store and picking out a cart with one wheel that squeaks and won't turn. Seventy-five percent of the year was good; but that other 25 percent made for a rocky ride. My absolutes, however, softened the daily, public criticism and helped me to focus on the positive side of that year.

Gradually I became more and more comfortable expressing my opinions, speaking to large audiences, and performing at a moment's notice. I knew that I had a safety net firmly in place. That net really had nothing to do with *what* I did, but had everything to do with *who* I was, and that made a world of difference in how confident I felt about everything I did. My comfort zone had grown, its borders now expanded to include some things I had always dreamed of and others I had never thought about before. I knew who my encouragers were, I knew what things activated me, and I had strong absolutes. I was feeling more like myself with every commitment I made to myself. Basically, I defined myself with those absolutes.

## THINK BEFORE YOU ACT, LEST THE PRINCE DOES TURN BACK INTO A FROG

Is there more strength in making strong decisions *before* the situation arises, or simply taking the "wait and see" approach? Do you stop and think first to see if your actions are really following your belief system? Many of us don't think too carefully in moments of great stress. One classic headline in the papers told of a news event in the Philippines: "Police Kill Man to Stop His Attempted Suicide." What kind of sense does that make? When a difficult decision has to be made, it is better to have already made the decision beforehand. The best way to fight the unknown . . . is with the *known*. And that's exactly what establishing your absolutes is all about. Fight fear and doubt with the peace and courage of absolutes. Get to know yourself and those around you. Discover *who* it is you can trust and *what* it is you can trust. That way, if the prince does turn back into a frog, at least you'll have a safety net to break the fall and help you bounce back.

Chapter 9

# DETERMINING PERSONAL ABSOLUTES

I like to think of my absolutes as ground rules. And ground rules are definitely needed before doing anything as risky as climbing out of the waters of your comfort zone to kiss the frog that has been madly hopping around trying to get your attention. Absolutes are entirely personal; each individual creates and adopts his or her own set of unwavering truths. Defining your absolutes is simple, but it does take a few minutes, or possibly days (depending on how chaotic your life is at the time!), to really think about. It's a good thing to do when you're swaying in a hammock on a beach in the Bahamas, but your breakfast table will do just fine too. Once you've committed yourself to them, you'll find that absolutes are life changing. To help you define your own personal absolutes, I'd like to share my top five absolutes in detail.

## ABSOLUTE #1: IN GOD I TRUST

I trust in God.

As a child, I remember my Dad pulling out a coin and

showing me what America believed: "In God we trust." But that wasn't all he did in this teaching moment. He then flipped over the coin and posed a thoughtful question: "Wouldn't it be great if we could put on the other side of the coin, 'God can trust me'?" That has always stuck with me. After all, I do want to be trusted—especially by God.

The United States national motto is significant and profound. Although Congress designated it as the national motto in 1956, the phrase "In God we trust" originated during the Civil War. Treasury Department records show that Salmon P. Chase, Secretary of the Treasury, received a letter from the Reverend M. R. Watkinson of Ridleyville, Pennsylvania, dated 13 November 1861. The Reverend wrote of religious sentiment in the Union and the need to acknowledge "God, Liberty, [and] Law." He felt that an inscription on the nation's currency that referred to God "would place us openly under the Divine protection we have personally claimed."

Secretary Chase agreed with the Reverend and asked that a motto be prepared for inscription on national coins. "No nation can be strong except in the strength of God, or safe except in His defense," Chase wrote. "The trust of our people in God should be declared on our national coins."

In 1864, Congress passed the first act that would change the composition of national coins and authorize the placement of a new motto: "In God we trust." The two-cent coin was the first to come out of the mint with this motto. In the years following, the motto disappeared and reappeared on several occasions until 1956, when Congress passed and the President declared "In God we trust" as the national motto. By 1966, the motto appeared on all forms of currency (see *Fact Sheet on the History of "In God We Trust,"* United States Department of the

Treasury Web site, www.ustreas.gov/education/fact-sheets/ currency/in-god-we-trust.html).

George Washington instigated many of the nation's official references to God. In 1789, as he took the oath of office to become the first President of the United States, Mr. Washington solemnly swore that he would uphold the Constitution. At the end of the thirty-five-word oath of office outlined in Article II of the Constitution, he added four words: "So help me God." Every President since has followed suit. No doubt he felt the tremendous burden of his new, unprecedented responsibility and searched for assistance then as he had many times in the past.

Today, however, critics are increasingly vocal about discrediting anything to do with expressing allegiance to God. Gordon B. Hinckley, best-selling author of *Standing for Something*, expressed his concerns about what he terms "the secularization of America":

'The single most substantial factor in the degeneration of the values and morals of our society is that we as a nation are forsaking the Almighty, and I fear that He will begin to forsake us. We are shutting the door against the God whose sons and daughters we are.

"I have heard Margaret Thatcher, former Prime Minister of Great Britain, say on more than one occasion, 'You use the name of Deity in the Declaration of Independence and in the Constitution of the United States, and yet you cannot use it in the schoolroom.' Her words are a rebuke and an indictment of America. Reverence for the Almighty, gratitude for His beneficent blessings, pleadings for His guidance, and a willingness to acknowledge His omniscience and omnipotence are increasingly being dropped from our public discourse" (*Standing for Something* [New York: Random House, 2002], xvii).

### Acting on Your Belief

An overwhelming 95 percent of Americans profess a belief in God (see Richard N. Ostling, "In So Many Gods We Trust," *Time,* 30 January 1995). Trust in a higher power is really the way most of us view our place in the cosmos. *Acting* on that belief is another matter.

In 1978, by the power of example, I learned how to act on my belief. My family was living in Buenos Aires at the time, where my father was working as an ecclesiastical leader for our church. His duties required a great deal of travel throughout Argentina, Chile, Uruguay, and Paraguay. When my two younger sisters and I were out of school on vacation (the older siblings were in college at the time), we would travel with him to visit other church members and people in need.

I remember well one trip when I was fifteen. It was Christmastime, and we had planned to visit the crystal blue lakes of Nahuel Huapi and the towering beauty of the Andes in Bariloche, Argentina, before crossing over to Osorno, Chile. It stands out not only because of the unforgettable beauty of that region, but mostly because we found ourselves in the middle of a war zone. This experience defined a large part of my life and my faith, and instilled in me the need to make trust in God my number one absolute. Years later I asked my dad to write down this experience. Because he is somewhat of an expert in Latin American politics (he lived and worked throughout Latin America for more than thirty years, beginning with his position as an executive for CitiBank), he was able to describe well the political climate of the region as we prepared for that trip in 1978. He tells the story better than I could, so I take the liberty here of sharing his letter. He wrote:

"Argentina and Chile had been very good neighbors for many decades because the Andes Mountains were such a natural and formidable border. However, way down south there was an area far beyond the Straits of Magellan where a border had not been defined to the satisfaction of either country. It is at the end of the Beagle Canal. Only a few rocks stick up above the waves. They are not really islands because no one can live on them; they are just dots on a map. But they did become important when it was believed that there was oil offshore. Both countries quickly claimed those three tiny dots. . . .

"During normal times, these two countries could have easily managed to settle this economic problem—some kind of joint exploration and development, for example— but 1978 was not a normal time. Both countries were under strong military governments. Chile had recently gone through a revolution. . . . Argentina was still working its way out of the effects of the dictatorship of Peron. . . . Both governments were hard-line military, had egos to maintain, and feared that if they were perceived as being weak on the border issue they would lose hold of their country's present and future. Each took a childish 'no flexibility' position and claimed all three little dots on the map just in case there proved to be oil out there under the continental shelf towards the Antarctic.

"Both governments decided to close and fortify their borders of 3,000 miles, especially in the south, down to the Straits and the Beagle Canal. I had heard about the problem, but did not think they would really close the borders. I thought it was just comic opera posturing. I was not well informed. I had a trip planned south, from Buenos Aires, Argentina, to visit our principal church districts in Argentina, then to cross the Andes into southern Chile and work our way up to Santiago. Meetings had been planned a year in advance, with many people involved. Before our family left Buenos Aires, the U.S. Embassy had warned all U.S. citizens that things looked dim and to avoid the border."

[In spite of the tensions in the region, Dad—who always trusted in God—assured us everything would be okay. He simply would not shirk his ecclesiastical duties, no matter the circumstance.]

"It was just unthinkable that we should back out and disappoint all the church members waiting for large meetings to renew their friendships and brotherhood with each other. As we came nearer to the border, after having outstanding success in all of our meetings along the way in Argentina, we learned that the situation between Chile and Argentina was becoming more and more tense. News reports said that troops were moving into place along both borders. . . .

"When we arrived in Bariloche, Argentina, we were told that the border was now totally closed. No one was allowed to cross. Our planned six-hour road trip in the family Suburban across the border through beautiful lakes and mountains to the waiting [church] members on the Chilean side would have to be canceled. Troops, guns, and even tanks were rumored to be in place. Shooting was ready to start if either side blinked. Civilians were ordered to stay away. I could not believe it nor would I accept it. It was simply not in God's plan. I knew that meetings had been canceled on other occasions because of blizzards, earthquakes, floods, and hurricanes, but this was an unbelievable, insignificant, childish test of military will by two stubborn governments. I truly felt that God would open the way. I felt no risk or fear to me or to my family.

". . . The family climbed in the Suburban and we took off on the highway which was paved most of the way, but gravel for 20 km (12 miles) between the last Argentine post and the first Chilean post. . . .

"My resolve started to weaken when we began seeing camouflaged Sherman tanks with those ugly big guns alongside the road as we neared the border. Then [Sharlene] noticed camouflaged troops lying in the bushes with their guns pointed towards us. Hey, this might get serious, I thought. Yet my instincts said to push on. A military roadblock appeared. The soldiers seemed surprised to see us and stopped us, but they had no orders to detain anyone coming from Argentina going towards Chile—only to shoot at anyone coming from Chile. They said we could go ahead but to forget trying to come back. Then another military officer stopped us. He wanted an explanation, but again he admitted he had no orders to stop us. We proceeded. We came to the last Argentine border position and there it was a different problem.

"At that position we normally would just present our papers and go through customs, immigration, police good conduct check, and so on. We would usually pay a fee of twenty dollars or so and drive on across after an hour of paperwork. This time, everything was closed tight. There were a few official people there, but they had no authorization to allow anyone to pass through. It was time for my final effort. Over the years I had found that prayer solves situations most of the time, but when it seemed nothing else would work I would try my last desperate maneuver. I pulled out my official and legitimate Salt Lake County Deputy Sheriff's badge. (Back in 1955, I had flown a single engine plane from New York to Buenos Aires. Part of my survival gear, in case of unexpected emergency landings in uninhabited jungle or desert areas, was a shotgun and a .38 revolver with birdshot shells to hunt food as well as to fend off angry bulls, alligators, or anyone without good intentions coming towards us. To carry the guns I had to join the Sheriff's Flying Posse and obtain a gun permit. The guns were disassembled and packaged in appropriate separate containers. But the first border crossings involved an awful lot of paperwork, lost time, red tape, lack of cooperation, etc. Then on one occasion, my sheriff's badge fell out on the floor. As I picked it up, the airport official asked to see it. He looked at it carefully, saw the words 'Deputy Sheriff,' and asked simply, 'Como John Wayne?' I nodded seriously, trying to keep back my smile. He had seen a lot of Western movies. With a gesture of welcome he said, 'Pase, colega, no hace falta mas papeles'—Go ahead, colleague, you don't need any more papers. After that, I always carried my Sheriff's badge in case just a little more authority was needed.)

"I showed the badge, the man was impressed, and he explained carefully that he could not stop me from going ahead into Chile, but that the Chileans were not likely to let us through, and he could not let us back into Argentina. We were truly going into no man's land. Nonetheless, I felt totally at peace and saw no risk because the Chileans were a peace-loving people and had no tendency to do anything violent. I thought that both the Argentine soldiers and the Chilean soldiers were reasonable and sweet people with some misguided leaders far away in their carpeted office suites. The thought came that as long as I drove slowly, prayed some more with the family, smiled, and nodded, and talked nicely and respectfully each time we were stopped we would go right on through. That is exactly what happened.

"We drove slowly through the dirt, seeing no one at all until we got closer to the Chilean side of the border. Then, we again saw soldiers in camouflage, guns pointed at us, and surprised looks. But there was no problem. At the border checkpoint, the officials were astounded to see a family of 'gringos' coming across the border.

"'Didn't anyone stop you?' they asked incredulously.

"'No,' we answered.

"'Didn't the Argentines stop you?'

"'No, they just told us we could not come back into Argentina.'

"The Chilean authorities questioned us for some time. They were both surprised and somewhat dumbfounded, but just shook their heads and let us on through.

"Perhaps I was stubborn, perhaps God really wanted those meetings held, perhaps our crossing helped defuse the border problem because each side was ready to shoot until a family came slowly through and it was obvious that there was nothing threatening to either country nor were they really wanting to shoot at each other. I prefer to feel that God is willing to answer our prayers, guide our thoughts, open doors, and influence people when our intentions are to serve Him and those about us."

### The Power of Trust

In today's world, where intellect and spirituality are often viewed as noncompatible, the idea of trusting in something unseen seems downright stupid. Many claim that if we can't prove it scientifically or measure it statistically or monitor it visually, then of course we must dismiss it. But the world really isn't that clinical, no matter how much others may insist that it is. Our souls, more than our intellect, still determine the course of our lives, the decisions we make, and how we feel about them. Because of that, we must acknowledge the character of the soul. What are the basic elements of the soul that make you more *like* me than *different* from me? The elements are indeed basic: life, love, and trust.

Some might say that to trust is fine, as long as you can see what you're trusting in. But trust isn't built on sight, it's built on *experience,* and through experience I have found that the most powerful trust I can have is a trust in God. Sight unseen. My first absolute lays the foundation for everything else, including my other absolutes. It supports my values and beliefs and strengthens my resolve to live by them. It gives me courage to live by a certain set of standards. Without that absolute, I'd have no resolve, I'd live according to my whims and pleasures, and I'd constantly wonder about my purpose in life. I would enjoy life sporadically and without real meaning. I would experience moments of happiness, but not much real joy. With this first absolute in place, I can move freely and confidently through the other absolutes, knowing I can always come back to that well of courage when I need another long drink.

## ABSOLUTE #2: DEFINING SUCCESS AND HAPPINESS BY RELATIONSHIPS

In elementary school I wore a lot of hand-me-downs and inexpensive clothing. And I remember thinking how great it would be to be rich. I watched others go on extravagant vacations and eat at McDonald's all the time while I ate the sandwiches my mom made us as we carpooled from one thing to another. I often used to think,

"Wouldn't it be something to eat out whenever we wanted?"

When I started wearing glasses and kids called me "four eyes," I wondered what it would be like to be famous and popular. I dreamed of someday being a "somebody" . . . somebody who others would want to sit next to, invite to parties, and claim to be friends with. I thought being rich and famous was the sure ticket to an ideal life. Fortunately, I got a taste of that at the young age of twenty so I didn't waste my life searching for something I would eventually discover to be one of the biggest hoaxes of all time.

I learned faster than most. But not as quickly as those who have cheated death or who have lost someone dear to them and thus experienced a defining moment or a "second chance." Anyone who has ever experienced a tragedy is never the same again. Everything becomes clear, priorities zoom into focus, and time can no longer be wasted on frivolous things.

But a tragedy or near-tragedy really isn't necessary for you to have a defining moment. It can happen right now as you sit there. Just take out a pen, put it on a piece of blank paper and write down, in order, what really matters the most to you, what you would miss the most if you had to give up everything you love and own. That's it. If you have half a heart and half a brain, you'll find that money and accomplishments aren't nearly as precious as loving and being loved. And then you might wonder why you're spending more time and energy on the priorities that are lower on the list than on the ones at the top of the list. And you might think twice when thoughts like these enter into your mind:

"But I *have* to spend sixteen hours at work each day or I'll lose my job!"

"If I just stick with it a little longer, I'll get that promotion, and *then* I can spend time with the family."

"I'm already at home with the kids all day long—I'm too exhausted to be their teacher too."

"I have to work to maintain my independence, to be my own person."

"I just golf once a week—I need some time to myself too! My parents are too old to even know I am in the room when I visit them."

These statements may seem like true and good excuses when you speak them, but do the actions they promote back up the priority list you just wrote down?

During the past fifteen years I've been interviewed a lot. There are few questions that I haven't been asked. But only once was I asked, "Do you have any regrets?" I liked that question. It made me think. And now, as I make decisions in my life, I ask myself, *A few years down the road will I regret how I handled this? When I'm on my deathbed what will I regret or wish I had done more of, or less of?*

The answers to the last question govern what I try to do—at all costs.

### Fool's Gold and All That Glitters

All of us have probably had a "fool's gold experience": we see something that glitters and shines and looks just like the thing that will bring us real happiness in life. We grab for it with enthusiasm and think we've made it—life will be great from now on. It's time to sit back and relax. But then things don't go just the way we thought they would. That glittery object or event or choice or person is just a façade. It is not the real thing—and reaching for it was merely a foolish attempt to strike gold. The real gold is still out there somewhere; but it takes more effort to find, more thought to acquire, and more faith to sustain once found.

When I get bogged down in the day-to-day chaos of motherhood and start longing for a few days of glamour and ease, I often remind myself about fool's gold and its glittery disguise. Being a mother, being a *parent*, is without a doubt the hardest job anywhere, especially when you're trying to do it right. And while it is sometimes difficult to see the immediate rewards of that "career choice," it is the only career with lasting and meaningful rewards.

About five years after I had turned down a high-profile job with NBC Sports so I could concentrate on my family, I was cleaning up my then-four-year-old daughter's attempt to pour herself a glass of apple juice. As I was down on my hands and knees mopping up the mess, I kept my eye on the pro-basketball game on the television. At one point, I looked over to the TV set just as the woman reporter came on. She was the woman who had been offered my job, and there she was looking glamorous and hobnobbing with celebrities . . . while I mopped. For a brief second I felt sorry for myself. *I could be there. I could be doing that. Was I crazy?* But then suddenly there was this picture in my mind of what my life would be like *without* the very people who had created all this work for me to do. Poof . . . gone! No more children. I felt sad and empty. I no longer felt the martyr; instead I felt intensely grateful that I had had enough wisdom a few years back to trade in money and recognition for relationships.

Sure, I had gone from $250,000 a year . . . to *zero*. But in my situation there really was no other option. I simply couldn't and *wouldn't* delegate my responsibility to raise the children I had brought into the world. There was no way I could travel all over the world *and* be a mom. Some people have jobs that allow them to do both; mine didn't.

I continue to stay involved professionally, but on an extremely limited basis—maybe five or six days a month, in addition to the work I do after the kids go to bed. There are too many other important things to do for my children: take notes at Monica's violin lessons, help Nicole with her guitar lessons, make cookies on Wednesdays, keep up with a rambunctious four-year-old son, read to each of them, read *with* each of them, play basketball, help them practice the piano, teach them the value of hard work, and . . . . I'm sure I left something out . . . oh yes, and be a partner to my husband, Bob, who thinks I'm going about eighty miles an hour too fast but gets a kick out of watching me try anyway.

### Accomplishment or Character?

Besides your relationships with others, how else can you *properly* define success? The answer to that question is found in the answer to this more important question: Is it more important what a person *does* or who a person *is?* What rules: accomplishments or character? The next time you read the obituaries, notice what comes first. Typically, the deceased is described as a "loving father, son, and husband" or someone who "was always positive no matter her struggles." The accomplishments, if listed at all, come later and even seem cold and distant, as if they didn't even matter.

Who you are is defined by what you stand for. I saved a newspaper article some time ago because it told of a significant action that generally passes unnoticed. Nobody's life had been saved, no great civil change had been undertaken, and there had not been a great upset in the Super Bowl. A man had simply made a choice to quietly give up a prestigious position so he could be consistent with what he stood for. And whether you agree with his religious convictions or not, the fact remains that integrity is at the heart of the issue here. The article from the *Oklahoma Times* reads:

"STILLWATER—Oklahoma State University students on Friday won their fight to see 'The Last Temptation of Christ,' but OSU regents lost their chief executive officer over the controversy. H. Jerrell Chesney resigned the position he held for 15 years after regents voted to follow legal and administrative recommendations and allow the movie to be shown on the Oklahoma State University campus next week. Chesney said he found no fault with the regents, saying their action to let the film be shown was 'under all the circumstances the right decision.' But he said he personally opposed the film, saying he viewed it as a 'false portrayal of Christ.' His resignation comes from his 'own personal loyalty' to Christ, Chesney said.

"Regents seemed stunned by Chesney's resignation. Board chairwoman Carolyn Savage wept while Chesney read his remarks. Later, regent Robert D. Robbins criticized faculty and students who brought suit against the regents because of the board's decision last month to delay the showing of the movie until regents discussed the implications of showing the film. OSU president Dr. John Campbell said Chesney's resignation 'came as a shock.' He said he knew Chesney had deep feelings about the film but that Chesney did not attempt to press his personal feelings on the regents or administrators" (Michael McNutt and Enid Bureau, "OSU Regents' Chief Quits over Decision to Allow Movie," 14 October 1989).

H. Jerrell Chesney determined that prestige and career were not number one on his list of priorities, no matter the consequences. There are probably a lot of people who would snicker at such a move, calling it inconsequential or pointless. But for someone who knows himself well enough to have absolutes that strong, such an action is anything but pointless. It reinforces that person's definition of himself, gives him more courage and, subsequently, greater joy and peace of mind.

### Who's Watching You?

While I covered college football I was often sent out on assignment to produce features on the nation's top collegiate players. One such assignment took me to Provo, Utah, and Brigham Young University, where I spent some time with Heisman Trophy winner Ty Detmer, who still had a senior season to play.

As we set up the lights and camera in his home, I noticed a poem under the glass covering his desktop. I could tell immediately that he was focused on things of greater importance than the potential millions of dollars he would make in the pros. I liked the poem so much (which carried no name to credit), that I asked him to fax me a copy soon after our interview. This poem offers another reason to choose a life of *real* value.

Words to Live By

There are little eyes upon you
And they're watching night and day,
There are little ears that quickly
Take in every word you say,

There are little hands all eager
To do anything you do,

And a child who is dreaming
Of the day he'll be like you.

You're the little fellow's idol
You're the wisest of the wise,
In his little mind about you
No suspicions ever rise,

He believes in you devoutly
Holds that all you say and do,
He'll say and do in your way
When he's grown up like you.

There's a wide-eyed little fellow
Who believes you're always right,
And his ears are always open
And he watches day and night,

You are setting an example
Every day in all you do,
For the little child who's waiting
To grow up and be like you.

We're all being watched—Heisman Trophy winner or
not. We all live a life of example of one kind or another.
Our choices will most surely have an effect on those who
live near and around us.

In defining success, your consideration must include
how you feel about personal integrity. Because your definition will be tested over and over again, maintaining
integrity is an essential part of making sure that your definition will not only work but also be effective. If you aren't
wholly committed to living by your definition of success,
it will be too easy to trade in your current struggles for a
more immediate and glamorous reward (money, status,
power, and so on). Like Mr. Chesney at OSU, do you have

the kind of integrity that would enable you to walk away from anything that detracts you from your definition of success and happiness?

Once you have established that you do in fact have the integrity to live by your definition, then go ahead and put it in writing. To help, ask yourself some of these questions: Is the greatest kind of success and happiness achieved through your professional or personal life? Living single or with a family? Having great wealth? Good health? Recognition and honor? And in what order? I think most of us probably find that we're happiest when we are in a loving relationship or a caring friendship.

Good relationships affect our performance and outlook on everything. This works conversely when relationships are poor. Relationships are first and foremost in our lives, whether we admit it or not. Any valid definition of personal fulfillment has to include them.

## ABSOLUTE #3: MY OPINION OF MYSELF IS MINE ALONE TO MAKE

In 1997 I went to my first National Speakers Association convention held in Anaheim, California. Because I knew only one person there, I was nervous about my place in this sea of nearly two thousand other speakers who clearly (I assumed) knew a lot more about the business of speaking than I did. Though I had been accustomed to speaking from the platform for quite a few years, I was new to the industry and there was much I did not know.

The convention was a three-day event filled with workshops and general sessions, but the part I most looked forward to was the hour or two reserved for a "Meet the Pros" session. At this workshop, each participant was

assigned twenty-minute sessions with three different professionals. The ballroom was full of tables at which we
could meet the pros and discuss the details of speaking in
a relatively intimate conversation—each table could seat
eight people. Before even arriving at the convention, I had
carefully reviewed all the professionals involved and had
pre-selected the pros I'd like to spend time with to learn
more about the business. I was assigned none of my top
choices, but that was okay because I figured I could learn
from *anyone* there.

I was early to this workshop, so I immediately went
over to my assigned table and sat down in the seat next to
the one the "pro" would sit in. As everyone arrived, I made
sure I had my pen and notebook ready. The session bell
rang, and our table "pro" began. "Let's get one thing
straight," he led in with. "You don't have to be an ex-
football jock or a former Miss America to be a successful
speaker. In fact, they don't even know *how* to speak."

I was anonymous at this table, so no one knew he had
just thrown a dagger at me. He continued. "Before I go on,
why don't we go around the table and have each of you
tell us something about yourself in ten seconds or less—
something about your personal history that sets you apart."
Then turning to me he said, "Let's begin with you. Tell us
about you."

Suddenly, I became the shy introvert I had been years
ago. "I'm a . . . mom. I, uh, have four children . . . and I
needed to get out of the house." "Is that all?" he asked. He
wasn't sure he had heard right. I paused. "For now," I
finally concluded, embarrassed. The rest of the session I
spent just listening and wondering if his opinion was
shared by the entire world. Though it had been roughly fifteen years since I had won the pageant, I still felt as if I

had to hide that fact in order to be seen as Sharlene and nothing else.

But after that workshop, as I rested for a few minutes back in my hotel room, I thought about what I was feeling, and then I thought of my absolutes, specifically this one: *my opinion of myself is not dependent on anyone else but me.* I realized I was being silly and giving other people and what they thought way too much time in my *own* thoughts. I smiled and decided that someday the professional I sat next to might hear me speak and then change his mind about such generalizations!

## A Critical Ingredient

I have learned that there is one critical ingredient in having a good enough opinion of yourself that you can pull yourself back up when others knock you down. It's an ingredient that is often overlooked by those who rate success in our day and time. But when you have it, your confidence in who you are and what you stand for is secure. The ingredient is integrity—an essential part of Absolute #2 as well.

During my junior year in college, I met a handsome young man who struck me immediately with his confident yet uniquely humble demeanor. In an hour or so of chatting with him, I was drawn to his quiet personal strength. He had a solid inner core that kept him from being distracted by all the craziness that usually goes on in college. I knew I wanted to be around him more, so naturally I was excited when he later called me up. By the third date, I was smitten. I carefully mentioned to my parents that I was seeing someone, and when my Dad asked for his name, I was prepared. "Bob Hawkes, and he's from

St. Anthony, Idaho. His parents' names are Blaine and Bonnie." I knew exactly what Dad was up to.

For many years, my Dad had been an executive with CitiBank. He had been responsible for granting loans worth millions of dollars. Before he approved any loans, he always did a lot of background checks on the potential borrower to ensure the highest probability that the borrower was not only good for his word but also capable of repaying the debt.

Now that Dad was loaning his daughter and not cold hard cash, he naturally had even more interest in making sure the intended borrower could pass a background check. Of course, Dad's version of a background check was a lot different from the ones he conducted at CitiBank. At first I was appalled to learn that Dad had been regularly asking his network of friends, and mine, about the men I dated. But later I learned to take it all in stride because I knew it was done out of great concern and love for me.

About four weeks after Bob and I began dating, I got a call from my Dad. Bob was over at my apartment at the time, so I went into the back room to chat with my Dad. I knew why he was calling. "So, can I keep him?" I teased Dad, pretty sure I had hit the jackpot. My dad was enthusiastic in his response. "Not only can you keep him, but your mother and I encourage you to! One woman I talked to said if she had a daughter, she would want her to marry Bob. Someone else said Bob was the hardest worker and the most trustworthy young man he had ever supervised. They used words like *integrity* and *wise* to describe him. So by all means, keep dating him. And bring him home!" I was sincerely pleased that I had my parents' approval. As much as I liked to believe that I was independent, head-strong, and had good judgment, I knew in the back of my mind that they had a unique kind of discernment that loving and committed parents always have. I had to admit that I depended on their judgment to help me in the most important decision of my life.

After our conversation, I went back into the living room where Bob was studying. I couldn't help but put him to the test. Just for fun, I wanted to see what his reaction would be when I told him that my Dad had been checking up on him. His reaction would tell me even more than I already knew. If he had something to hide, he would be appalled. If he was sure that his conduct had always matched his words, he would not be offended.

"How are your Mom and Dad?" he asked casually when I walked back in. I reported that they were fine, and then I blurted it out. I told Bob that my Dad had spoken with people who knew him well, even some of Bob's past supervisors, and Dad had called just now to let me know whether or not it was okay to keep dating Bob. I watched for his reaction carefully. He laughed. He just laughed! "So what did they say about me?" His curiosity begged for an answer. I was relieved that he was neither offended nor appalled. Bob was so sure of who he was and what he stood for that he was completely comfortable with any kind of personal questions. He knew he had tried his best to live his life with integrity. His opinion of himself had been settled long ago when he decided that integrity would be central to all his thoughts and actions. He could relax when someone went delving into his past.

You might not feel comfortable knowing that someone else is performing a background check on you. But you can feel comfortable with yourself and your own personal integrity starting right now. Begin by building on your positive qualities until you eventually reach a place within yourself that feels grounded in good principles of living.

### Follow Your Gut Feelings

I have found that even though I have developed a good general opinion of myself, I still doubt specific feelings I have and choices I make because I let the opinions of others sway my thoughts, whether just for a few moments or for greater periods of time. The older I get, however, the more I tend to trust my own "gut instincts." But not always. And every time I lapse into the rehearsed self-speech—*But they know more than I do, so I shouldn't ask any more questions and appear stupid or untrained*—I end up wishing I had stood up for myself and my opinion.

A classic example is the time I had to go helicopter skiing. Yes, *had* to. I was putting together a feature report for the World Alpine Championships in Vail, Colorado, and my assigned producer thought we should shoot a quick one-and-a-half minute piece on the excellent helicopter skiing conditions in the surrounding Rockies. It was a great idea and would make beautiful video footage. I just assumed I would be narrating the piece and not actually have to do any extreme skiing.

So when my producer informed me that I would be flown to the top of a formidable, virgin mountain, dropped off with eight expert skiers, and left to find my way home, I asked a simple question. "Is there an easy way down?"

"Oh sure, there always is," he answered back without much thought. I didn't want him to think I was a wimpy skier, so I accepted his answer even though I had a lot of concerns and didn't really trust him when he said there was an easy way down.

The day for shooting came—a spectacular day for tap-ing Vail's backcountry and the surrounding white-topped peaks. The pilot landed the helicopter on a wide, flat open meadow. As I jumped out to get my skis on, the thought came to my mind that I should confirm the existence of an "easy route" before I let the pilot get out of my sight. But I wanted to blend in with all the experts, and they all seemed so thrilled and excited to be there, so I dismissed the thought. The snow looked good, there seemed to be a wide, almost groomed run right in front of us, so I said nothing. *Surely, they know a lot more about this than I do. And they all know I'm only an intermediate skier, right?*

My producer told us to all ski away from the camera just a few feet so they could get some shots, and then I could come back and either go down the easy way or grab the helicopter back. *I'll just ski on this easy part, and then I'll check with the actual head of the group to make sure I'm going down the easy way since I don't want to follow the others down,* I thought to myself.

The snow was slightly crusty but not too bad as we skied en masse a little ways. Just as I took off my skis to hike back and chat with the producer, I saw the helicopter taking off. *Great,* I thought, *there goes my easiest way down.* When I reached the crew, my producer explained that the pilot had other commitments and couldn't stick around. I turned to the group leader and asked if he could point me in the direction of the easiest way down. He looked stumped and then told me that as far as he knew, there *was no easy way down.* I turned to my producer who suddenly looked a bit nervous himself since he wasn't nec-essarily an expert skier either.

We had no choice but to stay with the group. Bringing up the rear, I could see that the others were making flying leaps off a cornice, then zigzagging down the steep incline to a stop where they watched the others coming down. It was either the rocks or the cornice for me. But I was not interested in leaping off any of them, so I slowly and carefully side-stepped my way down around them. Once I got into the open and on a more manageable incline, I felt brave enough to actually point myself down the mountain and start to ski. Immediately, my skis broke through the one-inch crust that had formed over the powder and I was suddenly skiing up to my knees in stuff I had never experienced before. I was thrown off balance and began to tumble. Just as I got the skis out in front of me, I finally slowed down and came to a crumpled stop. I noticed with a quick tightening in my stomach that I had stopped just a few feet from a big drop into a gully filled with rocks.

I looked around for the other skiers and saw them on the other side of the slope looking at me with a mixture of concern and annoyance. Because our crew was still behind (and I fervently hoped that they had not been taping my descent), I waved for the others to go on. To make a long story (roughly three hours) short, I eventually made it down the mountain. But I had to dig myself out of big drifts at least four times, and my noodle legs were shaky and exhausted. My producer stayed with me all the way down, and I was embarrassed that I had to be baby-sat. I kept telling myself as I alternately side-stepped or traversed my way down, *Why didn't you listen to your concerns that this might be way over your head? Why didn't you ask more questions? Why didn't you take charge of your own events? Why didn't you value your own opinion on the matter?*

I had avoided expressing my opinions and doubts because I had wanted to appear more knowledgeable and skilled than I actually was. Instead, my plan backfired, and everyone found out I was considerably *less* knowledgeable and skilled than they had originally thought.

It's okay to express concerns, ask questions, and share thoughts. One individual's opinions are just as valid as the next person's. Naturally, there should be a lot of thought given to your opinions before broadcasting them (you can imagine the personal embarrassment that can occur if *no* thought is taken!). Others may in fact be a great deal more educated than you on one matter or another, but your perspective is still completely individual and important. The more you value your own opinion concerning specifics, the greater your opinion of yourself in general will become. And, once again, that's precisely when your comfort zone will grow.

## ABSOLUTE #4: I WILL ALWAYS AIM FOR BIG DREAMS AND EXCELLENCE

As a teenager, I remember being so taken by well-written motivational ideas that I would copy them onto poster board and then place them around my bedroom. For years I looked at the same quotes, and now as I look at them I realize that I have indeed internalized them. I suspect my own children will get sick of them soon. Some of the quotes include:

"Who aims at excellence will be above mediocrity; who aims at mediocrity will be far short of it" (a Burmese saying).

"Shun idleness—it is a rust that attaches itself to the most brilliant metals" (Howard Bearden).

"Happiness is a true goal of man, but it comes through striving, not through drifting. To halt, to be satisfied, is, in part, to die. Life is an adventure and can be glorious, but not for the parasite" (Dr. Ray Lyman Wilbur).

I have added my own personal quote/motto to these greats, although it is certainly not well-written or terribly profound. But I live by it anyway. My quote is:

"Dream big, dream often" (Sharlene Hawkes).

See, it's quite simple. I think daydreaming is a positive thing. As far as I'm concerned, if you're not dreaming, you're not living. You're just existing. I know that a lot of kids (as well as us big kids) get in trouble for too much daydreaming, but the right amount of it is where success actually begins. If you don't have enough hope in your heart to daydream, then how will reality ever be any different? The more you daydream, the more ideas you will give birth to. The more ideas you have, the more hope you will have. When hope is present, then fear takes a back seat. And when fear isn't in the driver's seat, you will have the freedom, even the personal permission, to accomplish anything.

I heard popular author and speaker Robert Schuller ask his audience once, "If failure was not a possibility, what would you do?" That's an enticing question, is it not? Would your goals change if failure was not a possibility? Would your approach to how you met your goals change at all? If so, then could it be that the *fear of failure* is dominating your intentions instead of your *dream of success,* or belief in yourself?

My good friend and mentor, the late Art Berg, wrote this about dreams: "Dreams are born in the heart and mind, and only there can they ever die." This thoughtful statement came from a man who had overcome tremendous odds to reach the height of the speaking profession. He had been selected by his peers to become the next president of the National Speakers Association before he suddenly passed away in February 2002. He had inspired hundreds of thousands, myself included, by his moving and yet surprisingly humorous perspective of life in a wheelchair. At age twenty-one, Art broke his neck in a serious automobile accident, leaving him a quadriplegic just weeks before he was to be married.

Art wrote:

"Our dreams, hopes, and aspirations are the essence of life. They give us courage and will. They feed, motivate, and inspire us to take risks, move forward, and meet our daily challenges. Our dreams are life preservers when the storms rage. It is a natural response, when faced with discouraging circumstances, to conclude that we will never realize our dreams. We sometimes feel overwhelmed by hopelessness. When I was struggling to find meaning during those first few hours and days after my accident, I was repeatedly cautioned by my doctor to keep my expectations low. I was warned against the alleged dangers of harboring a sense of false hope.

"I do not believe in false hope. I only believe in false hopelessness. For all medicine knows today, I believe there is more we do not know. Hope is the fuel of dreams. Hope is the brother of faith and the strength for tomorrow. Dreams are born in the heart and mind, and only there can they ever die.

"Lying in that hospital bed in Las Vegas, I wondered where all my hopes and dreams had gone. I wondered if I would ever be made whole again. I wondered if I would work, get married, have a family, and enjoy any of the activities of life that had previously brought me such joy.

"During this critical time of natural doubts and fears, when my whole world seemed so dark, my mother came to my bedside and whispered in my ear, 'Art, while the difficult takes time, the impossible just takes a little longer.' Suddenly, a once-darkened room filled with the light of hope and faith that tomorrow would be better" (Art Berg, *Finding Peace in Troubled Waters* [Salt Lake City: Deseret Book, 1995], 9–10).

Art turned adversity into opportunity and joy like no one else I have ever met. A year and a half after his accident he married the same beautiful young woman he had originally planned to marry, and for seventeen years they enjoyed a wonderful family and two beautiful children. Art became president of Invictus Communications, he was named Young Entrepreneur of the Year for 1992 by the Small Business Administration for a six-state region, and in 1998 he was named Consummate Speaker of the Year by the Keynote Speakers Bureau in San Francisco, California. In 1994, Art was featured in *Success* magazine as one of the Great Comebacks of the Year. As a member of the National Speakers Association, Art was awarded the coveted CSP designation (Certified Speaking Professional)—a status achieved by fewer than seven percent of professional speakers. He was also a world-class wheelchair athlete enjoying a variety of sports. On July 10, 1993, he set a world record by becoming the first quadriplegic at his level of ability to race an ultramarathon of 325 miles between Salt Lake City and St. George, Utah. He was one of the most successful and sought-after speakers in the world for a very good reason: he turned dreams into reality.

Of his success, Art wrote: "These are dreams that have come true for me. They came true, not in spite of my circumstances, but, perhaps, because of them" (ibid., 11).

## It's All in the Way You Look at Things

If you paid attention to the 2002 Winter Olympics you probably remember the unusual circumstances in which short-track speed skater Steven Bradbury won Australia's first-ever winter Olympics gold medal. Basically, he won because he never gave up and was the last one standing to grab the gold.

In 1994, Steven had been a member of the bronze-medal-winning relay team, but that same year in a World Cup race, he cut his leg badly, needing 111 stitches and losing four liters of blood. Four years later, he broke his neck crashing into the boards during training. Still, he came back to short track—a sport that has been compared to roller derby on ice. He entered the 2002 Olympic final ranked thirty-fifth in the world and was expected to finish well behind the pre-race favorite, American Apolo Anton Ohno.

Coming into the final turn, Bradbury was skating dead last. Suddenly Ohno was clipped by a Chinese skater, which sent the four frontrunners to the ice in a heap. Bradbury, moving "slow and steady" comparatively speaking, glided across the finish line first, much to his amazement.

Endurance really is a mental game. And it depends largely on the perspective you choose—fears or dreams, cowardice or courage, doubts or faith. Which perspective do you allow to dominate your thoughts? The direction you steer those thoughts is likely the same place to which all your energies—mental, physical, and spiritual—naturally flow. Consequently, all your abilities to make things happen for you will depend on whether or not those energies, those thoughts, are positive or negative.

### Be a Thinking Person

What do you think about when you don't have to think about anything? I recall walking home from track practice one afternoon in high school and just letting my mind wander. After a while, I started thinking about something I had read in the Bible: "As [a man] thinketh in his heart, so is he" (Proverbs 23:7). For the fun of it, I decided to divide up my thoughts percentage-wise to see what I thought about most and what I therefore might become.

To my amazement, I found that roughly 60 percent of the time I was thinking about a cute boy I had a crush on! About 20 percent of the time I thought of schoolwork; 10 percent of the time I thought of volleyball (my favorite sport at the time—and it was volleyball season); and the remaining 10 percent was filled with miscellaneous thoughts. I decided that I needed to spend my free-thinking time on more noble thoughts that might actually help me become a better person.

Thoughts are indeed powerful. I was fifteen when I learned just how effective thoughts can be in learning, even with something like a swimming stroke. I swam for the Lincoln High swim team, and my preferred events were the 50-meter backstroke and the 4x50 meter medley, in which I swam freestyle. But what I really loved was the butterfly. I couldn't do it, but I loved to watch other competitors swim the fly. It seemed like such a smooth stroke—it reminded me of dolphins emerging from the water then submerging again. But I knew that under the water, swimmers performed a tricky, almost syncopated, coordination of arms and feet. I really wanted to learn how to do it myself.

My coach tried to teach me first. But she soon gave up and told me to work on what I was already competing in.

Then I talked one of my friends, who was also the best swimmer on the team, into teaching me. Elizabeth Halouzka had the best butterfly stroke of anyone our age. It was seamless and powerful.

She was very patient with me, and for the longest time she gave me pointers each day at practice. But nothing happened. I was swimming like an elephant—just belly flopping, floundering, splashing a lot, and not really going anywhere. One particular Friday afternoon, I went home so frustrated that I couldn't stop thinking about that silly stroke. As I lay in bed that night, I kept replaying in my mind what I was doing wrong. I cringed as I saw myself splashing around. Then I replayed what Elizabeth looked like as she swam the butterfly. I couldn't go to sleep as I kept replaying her stroke over and over. I soon found that I could put the "film" I was watching in my head on slow motion so I could better analyze what she was doing. I could even pause it, put it on rewind, and play it again.

The next night I found myself reviewing that film again and, finally, it clicked. I began to envision *me* as the one swimming such a beautiful butterfly. I really felt like I knew it, and I could hardly wait until Monday to try it out in the pool. I then practiced again in my head on Sunday night.

Monday after school I ran to the pool and was the first one in. I immediately swung both arms around and into the water, gave a little kick, then did a big kick while pushing my hands into the water at the same time, which propelled me up and out of the water to swing my arms around again. I did it! I couldn't believe it! I swam a whole lap of butterfly strokes, and by this time my coach had arrived and come over to greet me. "When did you learn how to swim butterfly?" she asked, quite a bit surprised.

"Over the weekend!" I laughed. I never did race in butter-fly events—I was always much better in the other events so that's where I stayed—but I learned something more valuable than the butterfly stroke that weekend. I learned how to harness my thoughts.

Dreaming is really where the seeds of success or failure are planted. Because our dreams impact our actions, we must be disciplined with our thoughts. We must make sure that we think about good and successful things, things that bring us joy. The more we control our thoughts, the more productive our actions will become.

### Dreams vs. Priorities

After I spoke to a large group of teenagers and college students a few years ago, I was asked, "What if your dreams aren't the same as your priorities?" That's a very good question. What if you put your entire heart and soul into a dream or a goal, but it doesn't coincide with what you know should be your priorities? For instance, a woman wants to take full responsibility for her children, but she has a dream of running her own business. What should she do? Or maybe a young man dreams of being an artist but also wants to bring in a steady income with a dependable "day job."

My personal rule of thumb concerning dreams *vs.* priorities has been to simply move full steam ahead on both. Sometimes your dreams and priorities won't interfere with each other but will work well side by side. When the two do seem to intersect and force you to take one route or the other, let your priorities have the right-of-way. Priorities exist, after all, so we don't lose focus on the things that really count, the things that bring us joy and satisfaction. Priorities are absolutes too. But just because you know that your priorities are where your allegiance lies doesn't mean you should give up your dreams. Perhaps it means you should come up with new dreams. But don't ever stop thinking or dreaming.

On occasion you might dream about accomplishing one particular thing but then encounter *opportunities* that lead you in other directions. What do you do in such a case? Do you put blinders on and plod forward toward a dream that has never opened a single door, or do you allow yourself the luxury—and the adventure—of accepting new and altogether different dreams that grab hold of your imagination based on those unexpected opportunities?

I never dreamed of being Miss America. And I never dreamed of working for ESPN. I never dreamed of being a professional speaker. I *did* dream of running hurdles in the Olympics. I also dreamed of finding Prince Charming and having a family. I dreamed of being a concert pianist. I dreamed of studying at Harvard or Oxford or Cambridge. I dreamed of getting an MBA.

Prince Charming and a family are the only childhood dreams I have realized, and I consider myself exceptionally lucky because of that. But am I a failure in everything else? What happened to me? Why did my dreams head in totally different directions? As I have analyzed my decision-making processes over the years, I have recognized a simple approach to my success: I have eagerly grabbed whatever opportunities came along simply because I didn't want to let anything slip away. I didn't want to wonder, "what if?" And I had always been taught by my parents to keep looking for those hidden talents inside me. Maybe there was, and is, a part of me just wanting to cover all my bases.

You can do the same thing. If someone gives you a chance, even if it is something you don't think you can do, just do it. Then see what happens. And don't wait until all the circumstances are perfect to accept the opportunity. My husband tells me there is a saying in Idaho: "If you wait for the weather to be perfect, you'll never have any fun." And here's a thought I saw up on the bulletin board at school: "Procrastination is the grave in which opportunity is buried." So take the plunge. Prepare as much as you can for opportunities that might come your way, then be ready and willing to move outside of your comfort zone and snatch up the frogs that hop right over to you.

### Be Prepared

As a feature reporter during the 1994 World Cup soccer tournament, I was sent to Boston for a preliminary game between Argentina and Greece. I was working on several stories and I knew that soccer superstar Diego Maradona of Argentina would be there, even though his playing status was questionable due to drug abuse problems. I had been told he was not accepting any interview requests, but even so, there was a shot I might be able to talk to him right before practice as the dozens of reporters were allowed to crowd on the sidelines. Sometimes the players would answer questions that were yelled out from this media pack.

My Spanish was rusty because I had had no reason to really use it much in the twelve years or so that I had been living back in the United States. I drew up a huge list of questions in English first, and then I carefully translated each one. I called my sister, whose Spanish was completely fluent, to make sure I had done it correctly. Then I memorized the entire page of questions so that if I did get a chance (which realistically was slim to none) to speak with Maradona, I wouldn't be fumbling.

The next week I was in Boston, and I checked again to see if Maradona would grant me an interview for ESPN. He would not. He was silent, knowing that the bulk of the questions would be personal. I kept trying to convince his publicist that since I had lived in Argentina, and was actually living there in 1978 when Argentina had won their first World Cup, I would be a better interview than most. The answer was still no.

Right before practice I grabbed our cameraman and followed the media down to the sidelines in hopes of getting at least one question answered. For thirty minutes, as the players warmed up and kicked the ball around, this pack of about fifty reporters and cameramen followed Maradona from side to side as he moved about. There were just too many, and he ignored us all. Then I got an idea.

I went to the opposite side of the field, where no reporters were hanging out, and no players either for that matter. But I knew it was just a matter of time before the ball would bring Maradona down to that area. Sure enough, here he came chasing down the ball not ten feet from me. I waved at him and yelled his name, trying to get his attention. When he looked up, I asked him in Spanish if he could come over for a few questions. He looked surprised to see a blond speaking Spanish.

Maybe that's why he came over—his curiosity. My cameraman immediately got into position, and I quickly started firing away question after question that I had committed to memory, not giving him a chance to leave. Every time he finished an answer, he would begin to move away, but my question would stop him. The other reporters saw what was happening and began to descend on us, but by then he decided it was okay to stick around. I kept asking and asking, not letting any of the other reporters step on my time with him. We got a ten-minute interview that was later aired in its entirety during the halftime of that match, something not even ABC, who was airing the games, could get. I had decided to be prepared *just in case,* and that's the only reason I could grab that particular opportunity.

How often do opportunities float in front of you but you are either not prepared or scared or distracted, or the opportunities themselves don't fit in perfectly with your plans? Cut that number down. Grab opportunities that come your way. They'll probably never come back again.

## ABSOLUTE #5: I WILL NEVER ALLOW FAILURE TO DEFEAT ME

One time, as I kept hammering myself over a stupid decision I had made and couldn't change, my wise husband told me, "You can't keep kicking a dead horse and then be surprised when it doesn't wake up."

Once a "failure" or a bad decision has actually taken place, that part is *over.* The next step is all about *reaction.* And all of us really have only two choices when it comes to how we react: react badly or react well. The failure itself won't change because it's dead and gone. And it's not failure that defines us anyway. Our *reactions* to failure, and to success for that matter, are what define us and show us what we're made of.

I remember watching a football game on TV one afternoon several years ago. It was probably the most poorly played game I had ever seen. Maybe it had something to do with the mud that a little rain was creating, but both sides were having a difficult time executing any successful plays. There were a lot of fumbles, and as you might imagine, it was a low-scoring, boring game. Afterwards, a sideline reporter asked the winning coach for his perspective on how the team performed. The coach replied with emphasis, "It's not how good you can play when you're playing good, it's how good you can play when you're playing bad, and we can play bad as good as anybody."

He hit it right on the head: it's how you react when things go wrong that matters; it's also how you react when opportunities come along. *React!* And react well.

William Arthur Ward said: "If we learn from our failures, we have not failed. If we get understanding from our defeats, we have not been defeated. If we gain wisdom from our losses, we have not lost."

## React Well

Whenever I read the paper and I see a story about someone who has chosen to react well to his or her tragedies and misfortunes, I save that article. I place it in my bulging files and am personally encouraged by the knowledge that if others can react well to circumstances I consider horrendous, then I certainly can too. This one, from the *Wisconsin State Journal,* was particularly encouraging.

"ELK MOUND (AP)—When Mike Hase began his recovery from an accident that drastically changed his life three years ago, the first hurdle he had to clear was allowing others to see him with one leg. Then, and only then, was he able to begin his life again. Although his goals would be limited, he dreamed of moving on. Hase, now 18, has done more than that. A 6-foot-4, 215-pound senior, Hase is a defensive tackle on the Elk Mound High School football team, which won its first seven games this season.

He doesn't play every down, but when his team needs him, he's ready to go.

"'Every doctor we have ever talked with said football is out, he will never play again,' said Hase's father, Mike Sr.

"Hase was struck by a car driven by a drunken driver as he stepped down from a tractor on Highway E in Dunn County a couple of years ago. '(During recovery in the hospital) I never imagined I would do a lot of things,' said Hase. Elk Mound head coach Dan Pedersen and others in the school district offered their support. Hase, then a sophomore, accepted Pedersen's offer to be a manager for the football team. But last fall, Hase decided he had stayed off the field long enough. 'I was pretty nervous the first few times,' he said. 'But I just did it.'

"Steve McCullough, a special education teacher in Elk Mound and an assistant football coach, began working one-on-one with Hase last year. 'It's a team sport, and we realized Mike has certain special needs that won't allow him to do all the things that every other football player is expected to do,' McCullough said. 'We tried to set everything with the goal that he will do everything with the team, because when he plays, he plays with the team.'

"Hase, who plays only on defense, does some drills with his teammates. When they work on offense, he goes inside and lifts weights. And while his teammates run sprints or perform other conditioning drills, Hase jumps on a stationary bike and 'runs' along with them. . . .

"Hase said one of his proudest moments came last November when he got in the game during the fourth quarter of the Mounders' 14–7 loss to Edgar in the Wisconsin Interscholastic Athletic Association Division 5 state finals at Camp Randall Stadium in Madison. 'He told us one of his goals was to play at the state football championships because when he lost his leg, Elk Mound went to state that year and he had to go in a wheelchair,' his father said" ("Youth Loses Leg, Not Desire," 25 October 1993).

In 1984, I clipped an article from *USA Today* about a seventeen-year-old high school senior who was gaining attention from Major League Baseball for his ninety-mile-an-hour fastball. The feat isn't too uncommon in baseball, but Jim Abbott was born without a right hand.

This young, left-handed pitcher was deciding whether to go straight to the pros (he had been drafted by the Toronto Blue Jays) or take a scholarship from the University of Michigan. Jim Abbott was a young man who had never considered himself handicapped. "I don't think there's anybody who's really handicapped," he told *USA Today*. "If you look at it as if you're handicapped, then you are. Until I started having these interviews, I'd completely forgotten I had only one hand."

Jim chose to accept the scholarship and went on to inspire countless baseball fans and non-fans alike with his ability to dream big and make it happen. In 1987, he was named the Golden Spikes Award winner by USA Baseball; in 1988 he was named the left-handed pitcher on *The Sporting News* college All-America team. He posted a 26–8 mark with a 3.03 ERA in three years at Michigan, was a member of the 1988 U.S. Olympic team, and received the Sullivan Award, honoring the nation's top amateur athlete. And then, as a sort of encore to his amazing amateur career, Jim was selected by the California Angels in the first round.

For nearly ten years, Jim Abbott fulfilled his dream of playing professional baseball, but of even greater significance was the message he sent to thousands who watched in awe every time he took the mound: *This is how I choose to react to my circumstances. You can react well, too.*

## Tough It Out

Learning to react well to tragic events and circumstances is vital. But what would you do if your life seemed to include one big failure after another? One of the country's most popular talk show hosts, who recently concluded a twenty-year run of her own show, spent years just "toughing it out" before she finally overcame a succession of failures. Early in her career, Sally Jessy Raphael was fired eighteen times, moved twenty-five times to look for new work, and at times fed her family with food stamps as they lived out of their car. She tried out for 142 commercial voice-overs . . . and never landed one. She lost a daughter to respiratory failure and nearly lost her son in an accident less than three weeks later.

Because local broadcasting jobs often did not pay well, Sally held at least two jobs most of her life. Even after she began hosting her own talk show, *Sally Jessy Raphael,* she would tape all day and broadcast her radio show at night. In Miami, for example, she hosted an hour-and-a-half show live each morning, drove to Ft. Lauderdale to host a talk show from noon to one P.M., then returned each night to Miami Beach to be a radio disc jockey. And with all that running around, she earned only $500 a week.

How did she do it? How did she get from there to here and the end of a two-decade run of her popular show? How did she get up in the morning enough times to eventually earn an Emmy for outstanding talk show host and then be honored by the National Association of Radio Talk Show Hosts as talk show host of the year (1992). How did she go from $500 a week to making more than a million a year?

She believed in herself. She had the courage to believe in herself when others wouldn't. Sally is a textbook example of defying discouragement, of never allowing failure to defeat her no matter how insurmountable the odds. Voltaire wrote that "Life is thickly sown with thorns, and I know of no remedy other than to pass through them quickly. The longer we dwell on misfortunes, the greater is their power to harm us."

In 1985, an eighteen-year-old girl applied to Stanford. On the application, she was asked to provide one word that best summarized her. Her word: *invincible*. Debi Thomas was accepted to Stanford. And in 1986 she went on to become the first black World Figure Skating champion. The next year her "invincibility" was put to the test. She lost at the U.S. Championships and then again at the World Championship. The following year, however, Debi returned to the national championships. For the first time in fifty-four years, a dethroned champion regained the United States figure-skating title. Failure certainly did not defeat Debi—she truly was invincible.

Today, Debi continues her quest for invincibility . . . as a doctor. After retiring from professional skating in 1992, she went to medical school at Northwestern University and earned her degree in 1997.

What is the difference between those who fail and are defeated, and those who fail yet persist? The difference is a simple matter of choice in answer to the question: how will I react? People who refuse to accept defeat choose to do the hard thing. They try again, or try something else. They certainly don't sit around feeling sorry for themselves.

How do I personally overcome my own failures? I

recite one of my favorite quotes: "Winners do what losers *don't* want to do." Then it's just a matter of time. For Sally Jessy Raphael, it took twenty-six years of great effort before she earned $22,000 a year. It takes time . . . and building the right team, or support system, to buoy you up in times of discouragement. And we all know what that is like!

## THE PAY OFF

Once you have put together your own "team," you will be ready to kiss that frog. The great thing about having absolutes on your team is that they *are* absolute. They can't miss the team bus or call in sick—they go everywhere you do and can never be left behind right when you need them the most. Why? Because if you have defined them *for yourself* (and by all means, feel free to borrow some of mine to get you started) then you own them and they are there to carry you when you can't carry yourself. I'm sure you know what it's like to not really feel brave at all. But when you see that opportunity out there—a slimy frog lazily sunbathing on a lily pad—you need to know that you are ready and "armed" with your absolutes to handle and adapt to anything: a frog that turns out to be a prince, or perhaps nothing at all. You might encounter disappointment or success but in either case, having absolutes gives you the confidence of knowing that you won't lose yourself in the process, and that you can adapt to anything.

Chapter 10

# REFRESHERS
# FOR THE MIND,
# BODY, AND SPIRIT

We all need a "well" to draw from when life gets tricky—even excruciatingly difficult—and demands that we quench our thirst and refresh our bodies and minds.

If you're like me, your absolutes take up a lot of room in the well and likely provide nourishment when needed. But sometimes I need other things to boost my spirits and keep me going. These things may not be absolutes in the same way that my belief in God is, but they are vital to my well-being. These extra helps are individual and unique to each person. My ninety-six-year-old grandma, for example, feels secure only when she is perfectly coifed. She never goes out in public without looking stunning. I, on the other hand, am typically content with a baseball cap pulled over my head. Grandma's definition of what it means to be presentable in public is different from mine, though I completely respect—and admire—my sweet grandma's determination to look glamorous no matter how old she gets.

In this chapter I'd like to share a few of my own vital refreshers. You may think they are just what you need to keep you going, or they may simply help you determine other things that you can use to provide refreshment in your life. At the conclusion of this chapter is a page on which you may formulate your five absolutes and your vital refreshers.

Most of my vital refreshers have to do with my health. Is there anyone who *doesn't* want good health? A healthy mind, body, and spirit leads to a *happy* mind, body, and spirit.

## A HEALTHY BODY

I gained more than fifty pounds with my fourth baby, and the only way I could lose the weight was to exercise regularly (I have to exercise four to six times a week now to keep it off—it used to be just three times a week) and eat healthy. Notice I didn't say *diet.* I never go hungry. In fact, I munch a lot. I just choose my munchies and my food carefully (licorice instead of a Snickers bar, for instance). People who don't exercise always have terrific excuses for not doing it. "No time" is a popular one. "Too tired" is another. But I've found that people in general always tend to make time for the things they *really* want to do.

Because I really want to exercise and to feel good, I find different ways to make the time to exercise. I plan kid-watching trades with my husband, or I exercise during "Arthur" while my four-year-old is distracted. Sometimes I work out late at night, or early in the morning. It has become part of my daily routine, and I have more energy and good health when I stick to my routine. I can also get away with eating the occasional "7'4" Chocolate Cake" served at my favorite restaurant. And besides, the time I spend exercising is the only time that I allow myself to watch my favorite TV shows that I have videotaped specifically as exercise rewards.

For anyone with questions about the specifics of exercising, health, or nutrition, my favorite all-purpose site on the Internet is: www.ihc.drkoop.com/wellness/fitness. It will take you directly to a "Fitness Center," and to a better way of living. Another site with excellent and plentiful documentation about the powerful effects of exercise in countering depression is the American Psychological Association's page at apa.org. In the line for "search," just type in: exercise+depression. I read a bunch of those articles and am now convinced that if I were a psychologist, the first thing I would have a new patient do is to bring her sneakers to our session. We'd both lace up and, while out on a brisk walk, we'd chat. I would agree to keep seeing that patient only if she (or he) committed to a consistent, even daily, exercise routine of some kind. *Any* kind. Walking around the block, going sledding, shooting a basketball. I wouldn't care. Physical activity makes a huge difference to the mind, the spirit, *and* the body.

## A HEALTHY MIND

Take the time to read, enroll in specialty classes, or do other smart things. It will make you feel smarter. No matter the routine of your days, no matter the simplicity of the role, find ways to extend your mind constantly. Think of ways to volunteer, to change a law, to make a difference. Write a letter to the editor or learn how to really use the Internet. Let change include, not exclude, you. Stay ahead of your children. Let them see you read and study and practice too. Go ahead and daydream about all the things you'd love to do, all the things you might do, all the things you could do, and all the things you will do. And don't worry about shorting out your brain.

Once when I reminded my eight-year-old daughter Monica that she still had twenty minutes of reading to do, she whined, "But Mom, I have used 100 percent of my brain already today!" You might *feel* like that too sometimes; but in reality, we barely use 10 percent (if that) of our brain's capability. Your brain can handle more than you've ever imagined. Keep feeding and teaching it. The brain may be half the size of a grapefruit, but it can record eight hundred memories a second without ever tiring. The brain retains everything it takes in and never forgets anything. It's a remarkable, barely used miracle inside your head. How much of it are you wasting?

I recently went back to school as a graduate student in organizational communications. During my first day in class, after an absence from academics of nearly fourteen years, I immediately decided that my brain was hopelessly behind all the others. I didn't take it personally—after all, it was my brain I was concerned about, not me. My brain had not had occasion to be exposed to this kind of critical thinking in a very long time and I knew (at least I hoped) that it would simply take some adjustment and a lot of extra studying to catch up. I even took notes on the terminology the other grad students were using in class discussions so I could be sure to be prepared for the next class.

After one year in the program, my brain (I continue to separate it from the rest of my persona until I am certain of its progress) is coming along nicely but is still a bit behind on the analytical side of things. The best thing about my whole experience, however, is that I love what learning, *just learning,* is doing for me! When you learn one new thing, suddenly a bunch of other things make deeper sense. Even if you're not delving into highly intellectual topics, just the act of learning something new is both enlightening and empowering. It makes you more capable and better prepared to accept new challenges.

## A HEALTHY SPIRIT

The spirit, or soul, is the one thing that makes each of us absolutely unique. Your soul can never be cloned. So it's the spirit that we each should pay the most attention to. People of all different cultures and religions make room in their lives for that very thing. Whether it is reading uplifting messages of hope or simply sitting still for a few minutes of meditation each day, the point is that they're making time to focus on the value of their existence.

My husband appreciates stillness so much that every morning when we have two pianos being practiced at the same time, he walks around with completely soundproof, huge headphones on. He looks a bit funny, but he does appear to be stress-free!

Read out of the Koran, the Talmud, or the Bible. Read good books that put your thinking in the clouds, not in the mud. Watch movies that do the same. How often have you left a depressing, crude, or extremely violent movie . . . and felt really wonderful about life and yourself? It just doesn't happen. Treat yourself to a multimedia blast of *encouragement* whenever it's your choice to do so.

In fact, here's a bold challenge and promise. Don't see or read any violent or pornographic films or books for one year. Replace that material with value-centered material. At the end of the year, you will have an increased desire to be surrounded by material of substance and true worth, and a decreased desire to have anything to do with superficial and base entertainment simply because you will feel much better with the former.

William L. Stidger said, "We all become like that with which we live, like that which we look upon, read, or hear. If we like beautiful things, we become beautiful in our spirit. Those who see to it that only beautiful thoughts are accepted as guests in their homes and heart, become beautiful through constant contact with high and holy thinking."

Add to that suggestion a dose of service. Ask yourself if there's a way you can do something about the problems in our world. Can you feed one hungry child or help one teenager quit smoking? Can you teach the lonely little boy across the street to read or help your elderly neighbor plant a garden? Can you give a few hours a week to your local homeless shelter or food bank? Even better, can you give a few hours a week to your own child? Chances are you can find a way to do one of these things. And when you actually do it, you'll be exercising your spirit.

## MAKE A LIST

Think about your own body, mind, and spirit. Think of the vital refreshers you need in your life to help you survive and succeed. Then think about the five things that must remain absolute in your life. Now add to them a list of positive statements that will help you draw from your well and rely on your absolutes. For example, promise yourself to:

- Treat others the way you want to be treated.
- Take the positive rather than the negative approach to things.
- Become someone who can be trusted.
- Be accountable for your actions.

- Be loyal.
- Remember that life is sacred and that freedom is worth dying for.
- Never stop learning.
- Strive to make a difference.

## APPLYING TEAMWORK IN YOUR PERSONAL LIFE

In my work with corporations and sports teams around the world, I have found that no matter the purpose of the group, each one is interested in one thing: being better. And interestingly enough, I noticed that the most common approach to becoming better—to challenging those areas outside the common comfort zones—is the same wherever I go: to become better, be more united.

In other words, success as a group is all about *teamwork*. Sports teams and corporate teams alike have manuals, handbooks, playbooks, and logos that clarify the expectations of each team member.

When our oldest daughter was about three years old, my husband and I decided that what worked for the corporate and the sporting world could work for us too. We wanted our family to be unified and consistent, with shared expectations about what defined us as a family so we could *all* become our very best. We wanted our children to grow up knowing exactly what our absolutes are—what we stand for and what we're made of, what we hope to accomplish and what we will fight to preserve, what makes us happy and what makes us peaceful. And so we made ourselves a book: *The Hawkes Family Book of Standards*. It's a simple three-ring binder that any of us can add to anytime we want, with all sorts of sections that call for us to think about everything from what our governing values are to our favorite family quotes; from who we want to induct into "the Role Model Hall of Fame" to our "House Rules and Consequences." All of our absolutes are in one place—in this book that sits prominently in our family room. It has become something of an heirloom since each of the children participates in its ongoing formation.

About two or three times a year we sit down with this book during our weekly "family night," and review the goals we set, both current and past. (We love to laugh at the cute goals that were set several years before, when the children were three or four—goals like "I will learn how to do a forward roll" or even more important, "I will be potty trained by the end of 1996.") We discuss changes in our house rules as the children get older; we discuss any new books they want to add to our "Favorite Books" section. And we enjoy having a tangible place to put everything that defines us. We could hand this book to a stranger and, within a few minutes, he could tell us who we are, both collectively and individually.

## WRITE IT DOWN

With so much confusion in the world, it is essential to your mental and spiritual well-being to have one source of support that is sturdy and cannot be blown about by the winds of change. Absolutes are powerful because they give you and me the courage needed to adapt to *any* change and to be firm when pulled upon. And all of us are pulled in many different directions. Some of the paths we might be pulled down are harmful to the soul and can lead us to believe that we must abandon who we are and what we stand for. When this happens we have no hope of fulfilling our dreams or expanding our comfort zones because we're too bogged down by problems in the swamp. So before confusion sets in and the waters become so rough you can't get to the lily pad to even approach the frog, sit down and define your absolutes.

I'll make it easy for you to do. Following are two blank pages for you to fill out, or even tear out if you like. One is simply titled "My Absolutes" and should be used to write down your absolutes and vital refreshers as fast as you think of them. The second sheet is titled "My *Prioritized* Absolutes." This is important just in case there comes a time when absolutes conflict. For instance, when my absolute about "dreaming big" appears to be moving towards a head-on collision with my definition of real success, then I can refer to my list of priorities and remember that I have already determined that *real* success (in my home and my relationships) is what I'm after. Naturally, that absolute will get the right-of-way. My "dreams" will have to slow down or change lanes.

## MY ABSOLUTES

These are the things that *absolutely* do not change, regardless of the change going on around or within me.

## MY PRIORITIZED ABSOLUTES

1. _____
2. _____
3. _____
4. _____
5. _____
6. _____
7. _____
8. _____
9. _____
10. _____

Now that you have written down a few absolutes, and hopefully even prioritized them, understand that while this will help you a great deal in finding the courage to do the hard things outside your comfort zone, it will not always be easy to carry them out. But don't forget the "whys" you used in determining those priorities. Every time I feel down because I no longer get to cover some of the big sporting events I used to, I remember the "whys." One in particular: My little son Jacob, almost five years old, came running up to me after preschool last spring, threw his arms around me, and said with his huge, dimpled smile and bright blue sparkling eyes, "Mommy, I love you so much that every time I see you, my heart pops out!"

I had determined years ago that my family was more important than being on television. That's why.

*Step 4*

# UNDERSTAND THE PRACTICAL POINTS OF LEAVING YOUR COMFORT ZONE

Things I Wish I Had
Known the First Time I
Tried Kissing a Frog

# Chapter 11

# GETTING OVER NERVES: FROM FEARFUL TO FEARLESS

Wouldn't it be great to have a personal trainer lead you through the difficult and confusing steps on the way toward your goals? At first you might think so. But in reality personal trainers aren't really that helpful because they can't actually *step* outside your comfort zone for you. You must take the first step by yourself—no trainers will be around to pick you up and lift you over the edge. And if that's the case, doesn't it seem unfair for someone to do all the work to get you to the edges of your zone? Those who *have* made it to the edges of their comfort zones know the truth in this. They also know that the most productive steps a person can take are the ones he thinks through on his own, even if it means facing a bevy of worries and fears. Most frogs, after all, are covered in warts. And it's best to be okay with the warts before you pucker up.

Step 4 of this book is designed to help you muster up enough courage to reach the shores of your comfort zone and all the frogs that are out there waiting for you. Later on this particular chapter will help you tackle one of the most common warts on a frog: the fear of standing before an audience (whether that audience is in a sold-out concert hall or your boss's office).

But first let's talk about why you picked up this book in the first place: you want to move outside your comfort zone. You're not happy being fearful about trying new things, challenging yourself, and facing the unknown. Even though we've covered a lot of ground up to now about preparing yourself to head outside of your zone, you want to know *specifically* what those first few steps look like. Well, those steps are similar to the ones you take while you are building a relationship.

## LET'S START DATING

It's easy to plan your way from the waters deep inside your comfort zone to the outlying swamps and lily pads if you think of the process as a *courtship:*

**First, flirt a little.** Pick a dream, then research it, approach it, ask questions, get to know all of its friends, and hang out in all of the places where that dream might be found. When you're not actually learning about it, spend a lot of time just thinking about it.

**Second, start dating.** Take a class or a seminar to see if you really want to pursue this dream. Do your best to really understand it. Focus in on the dream and not on your limitations. Spend some money on a few items that can help you better understand your dream (i.e. buy software, books, etc.). Plan for future activities. And continue to think about it all the time.

**Third, get serious.** Now that you're spending a lot of time entertaining your dream, begin writing down a specific plan of action. Gather the opinions of others, especially the people you respect and trust. Don't get stuck in a rut, however, and let things drag on—give yourself a time-line to "fish or cut bait."

**Fourth, make a commitment.** Do whatever it takes to seal the deal: submit the appropriate papers, get the loan, announce your intentions to those you care about. Establish a start-up/completion date. Sign the dotted line. Work hard. Stop thinking so much and start doing. The difference between just being involved and being committed is like the difference between ham and eggs. When you see the eggs, you know the chicken was involved. When you see the ham, you know the pig was committed.

While flirting is lots of fun, commitment is where the action is and where *real* growth takes place and allows success to happen.

Still, courtship—and the lifelong commitment that inevitably follows—is a scary thing. Many people actually *base* their actions during the early months of dating on their fear of commitment alone. For many of us, a similar phenomenon happens when we reach outside of our comfort zones. In fact, comfort zones are most often defined by our fears. If your specific fear is impeding your options for success in the category you are striving to conquer, then that fear must be addressed, because fear will never allow you to reach excellence, only mediocrity. (My fear of leaping out of an airplane, however, has nothing to do with any of the real things I would like to accomplish in my life. Therefore, I have no need to challenge that fear. Besides, I have a motto: "If at first you don't succeed . . . then skydiving is not for you!" That keeps me from doing anything rash.)

## TAKING THE STAGE

The barriers of your comfort zone are expanded only when you are willing to take chances. More often than not, one of those chances will involve speaking publicly (or privately, but with someone in authority over you). If you are like most of the world and are overwhelmingly afraid of public speaking, it's important that you tackle the finer points of moving from stage fright to stage presence *before* you actually appear on stage.

Why is "stage presence" important to an entrepreneur or a business man or woman climbing the corporate ladder or the president of the local PTA or even a mom trying to convince her children that it pays to follow the rules? That's easy. Your stage presence in front of potential customers, critical investors, cautious superiors, and even your own always-observant children creates a lasting impression of how capable you are as a business owner, employee, PTA president, or parent. In a competitive world, you can't afford to lose a client—or lead a child astray—simply because your competition (and for you moms and dads, don't discount the entertainment industry as hungry competitors for your children's minds and morals) appeared more at ease presenting their proposal than you did.

In business, and in practically every other situation imaginable, presentation does matter. In our image-conscious world, a perception of inadequacy can cost you a great deal.

Whether you regularly speak to large groups or only occasionally say a few words at small gatherings, stage presence is essential to maintaining a professional image. Even if you are an expert in your field, people may assume you are ill-informed if you look uncomfortable.

So what is stage presence? It's the ability to appear before a group of people and command their attention as though you were welcoming them into your own home. It encompasses how you walk, how you stand, how you look at people.

But don't fret. Stage presence is a skill that can be acquired. Sure, some people are born with it. Others—myself included—have learned it. Like most people, I feared public speaking. If it weren't for my even greater fear of being cowardly, I never would have pushed myself to do the hard things—like saying yes when asked to speak instead of uttering a hasty no.

Here are ten steps to help you make the transition:

### 1. Make an Entrance!

Whether you are walking onto a large stage to make an introduction or simply moving to the head of the boardroom to make a presentation, your entrance will speak volumes about how much you believe in yourself. How you walk can convey confidence *even if you don't feel confident.* Conversely, how you walk can also give the impression that you lack self-confidence *even if you do feel confident.*

To master the appearance of confidence, ease, and comfort as you make your entrance, do the following:

**Breathe deeply and consistently before the entrance.** It's surprising how many of us forget to simply breathe. Air is free, after all, and oxygen has a very positive effect on the brain. As you wait your turn, breathe deeply to help ease the tension that mounts before any type of performance. I once had a voice teacher who would stop me quite often in the middle of a song just to ask me to breathe. At first I thought his request was strange because I was obviously alive and well. But it didn't take long for me to understand that my breathing was shallow and therefore unproductive. When I didn't take adequate breaths, my tone sounded thin and my pitch wavered. Sometimes my teacher would ask me to just sit with my eyes closed and breathe as if I was in a very deep sleep. And no, he wasn't a hypnotist. He just wanted me to understand what a really good, deep breath felt like. It feels comfortable and immediately relaxes your body, especially the vocal chords. So breathe.

**Stand straight.** There's nothing like a straight back, sucked-in stomach, and tucked-in buttocks to project confidence. ("Tucked-in buttocks" simply means that you "roll" your buttocks under your pelvis. This places your profile in a straight line instead of leaving your buttocks hanging out like a toddler's diaper!) Posture is important for both men and women. Women often round their shoulders, which makes them look depressed, and men often hang their heads, which has the same effect. Very few people actually pay attention to the importance of posture, but how you carry yourself could make you appear younger, stronger, happier, more productive, and here's the clincher, more *important* and *in charge.*

**Move with purpose; don't stroll.** Strolling makes you appear tired, and certainly not excited about the presentation. Besides, when you move with energy it will transfer to your voice and you will *sound* more energetic. Right before I walked out onto the massive Miss America stage in front of over 100 million television viewers, I felt weak. My legs felt like noodles—how could they possibly carry me? So as I stood in the wings I did exactly what I used to do before running the hurdles in a track meet: I hopped around, shook out my arms and legs, stretched and flexed. I got a lot of funny looks, but my energy level was ready to match the rush of adrenaline as I hit the stage. I moved out quickly and purposefully.

You may not always have "stage wings" in which you

can hop around privately, but you can take your mind off your nerves by *imagining* you are full of energy and ready to move out. When it's your cue, you must project more energy than usual, or you will appear listless and weak. You must be bigger than life—your voice needs to be stronger, your smile a bit bigger, your gestures just a tad more deliberate.

In my seventeen years as a TV sports reporter I have found that when I exaggerate my enthusiasm, the audience perceives my energy level as just right. If, however, I speak in my usual conversational tone, and let my face remain in the same standard expression I might carry throughout the workday, I come across as uninterested, tired, and even bored. Much is lost when a scene is transmitted through a camera, and the same effect occurs when your presentation is delivered from a stage, or even at the head of the table. Space, even just a few feet, swallows the energy you send out. Overcompensate, and you'll match the expectations of your audience.

### 2. Make Eye Contact

In one-on-one interaction with others, eye contact is a critical component of establishing trust and receiving immediate good vibes about a person. The same thing is important when interacting with a large audience. Make sure that you look to the right, to the left, to the far back, to the front row, and way up to the balcony. When you include everyone in the audience *continually*—not in quick, furtive movements, but sincerely and gracefully— you accomplish the same thing that a strong handshake and solid, up-close eye contact do.

Eye contact, however, can be difficult if you are trying very hard to remember your presentation. When you make eye contact, you might become distracted. When I first began speaking and performing, I found it too difficult to look at people right in the eye because it would throw me off and I'd lose track of what I was saying. So, I looked at the tops of heads. I would look over the room and find all different kinds of heads: bald ones, big hair ones, toupeed ones, dyed ones. It *looked* as though I was making good eye contact with everyone in the room; and I was the only one who knew I hadn't looked at a single eyeball. That helped me while I was learning to be comfortable on stage. Now that I am perfectly comfortable in what I do, I love to look at as many eyeballs as possible.

### 3. Practice Your Million-Dollar Smile

Remember to *smile!* Unless you are delivering tragic news, keep your face pleasant when you're in front of a group (that means corners of your mouth slightly turned up—you will feel weird, but to everyone else you will appear pleasant). Don't let your mouth sink into the natural frown position while you wait your turn to speak. Maintain a pleasant look even when you're not saying a thing.

Smiling gives the impression that you are in charge, comfortable and knowledgeable, approachable, and able to relate to others in the room. Even though there may be things for you and the audience to be concerned about, smiling will disarm them, loosen them up, and put them at ease. By the way, one giveaway of someone who is overcome with nerves is a "dead" face—in other words, a face so lifeless he is obviously "scared to death." Even a serious person with a serious topic can show confidence with a touch of animation.

### 4. Take a Stand!

If you must be on stage but won't be speaking or performing (at least for a while), don't fidget! Most people are not aware that they fidget. They rub their hands together, pick or look at fingernails, bounce their legs, tap their toes, and so on. Such actions are extremely distracting and a quick way to announce a bad case of nerves. If you are obligated to stand for a while, stand quietly. Be aware of your hands—don't hold them together down low in the "fig leaf" position and don't cross your arms in front of you (it looks defensive). Either keep your hands to the side, or held together behind you, again watching your posture.

Once you are speaking, move your hands as you would if you were talking to friends. The more free you are with your arms—that is, letting them move *away* from your body from time to time—the more comfortable you will appear. A good way to decide if you are moving too much or not enough is to record yourself on video. At first you may feel uncomfortable knowing that you are being taped, but stick with it. Try it several times and you'll notice a difference each time. You are usually your best critic as you view the recording.

As you stand, pay attention to your stance. Again, this is something you may want to record and then look at from a semi-objective point of view. Men, stand with your feet slightly apart, not in a wide army or "jock" stance. Women, do *not* stand like a ballerina in first position. Yes, ballerinas are graceful, but that first position makes anyone look like a penguin at attention. Do stand with feet parallel and slightly apart, or better yet, with one foot slightly in front of the other, the heel of the front foot about 2 inches away from the middle of the back foot, and the back foot pointing towards 10 or 2 o'clock, depending on which foot is in front. The shoulder that corresponds with whichever foot is in front should be *slightly* angled out front as well. (This last position is actually the best one of all because your silhouette slims by about ten pounds. Women, this position is an absolute must when pictures are being taken. And speaking of pictures, both men and women must think about sucking in their tummies.)

### 5. Learn the Art of Just Sitting

If you are sitting, maintain a dignified, straight back. This is not to be confused with the unnatural sitting position of a West Point cadet, just a relaxed but *not* slumped position. For men, legs are generally crossed or parallel (about 6 inches apart). When on stage, however, do away with the wide version of crossing—that is, the ankle resting on the knee. It looks too casual (even in a casual setting) and unsophisticated.

Women have two options: one, keep knees together and pointed slightly in the direction of the focus of attention, with ankles crossed (this can get tiring but it does look elegant), or two, cross your legs but DO NOT leave the foot of the crossed leg floundering out in space somewhere. Move the planted foot in the direction of the floundering foot and then gently rest the top leg on the planted leg. If you are wearing heels, this will be much more comfortable than if you are in flats or sneakers.

For both men and women, hands should rest in a relaxed palms-together clasp in the lap, or one hand palm down with the other resting (palm down) on top of that hand. Another option is to clasp hands, with your fingers intertwined, and gently wrap the top knee of the crossed leg.

When you appear elegant on stage (even though that

may not be your persona or "style") you project calmness, dignity, sophistication, and complete control.

### 6. Learn to Handle a Microphone

If you are using a lavaliere microphone—the wireless, hands-free kind—*always* check two things. Make sure there are fresh batteries in the transmitter (that means that brand new batteries go in right before you are to speak), and personally check to see the button is pushed to "on" and there is a little red light glowing. That will tell you everything is in working order. Since audio technicians control your audio, you don't need to worry about being heard as you wait backstage, but do keep in mind that sometimes technicians make mistakes and they might leave your microphone on. There have been many times in my business when a microphone is left on as the unsuspecting carrier visits the *restroom*. You can imagine the entertainment that provides for those wearing the headphones!

Usually, however, the audio technician will make sure your audio level is up only when you step on the stage. (It is always best to speak to that person beforehand though, just to make sure they know what you look like and what your cue is so your microphone will be on before you say your first word.)

If you will be holding a microphone with a cord, don't play with the cord. Don't wrap it around your fingers. That's another clue that you're nervous. Leave it alone; it's not a security blanket. Only hold it when you actually need to move it out of the way, or it gets caught as you are walking. I know that in the old days, lounge lizards would often close their eyes and caress the cord in their hands, but that is definitely passé. Use your free hand to gesture with. And by the way, do keep a free hand. Two hands on the microphone is overdoing it and makes you look desperate to hold onto something.

If you have been handed a wireless, handheld microphone, just check to confirm the lever is in the "on" position and that the red light is on. When you are working with a microphone, make sure that you keep the microphone head about one inch from your mouth and never let it stray. If the volume constantly changes because your mouth strays from the microphone head, your audience will concentrate harder on the one word they missed than on your message. You will project professionalism if you glue that microphone to your chin (you may want to take me literally if you have a problem with this) and keep it there, just one inch from your mouth no matter how animated you get, how much you turn your head, or how tired your arm gets from holding it there. Don't let that arm drop.

At just about any large meeting or dinner, there is a podium behind which everyone on the program is obligated to stand for cover. Don't lean on it, and don't stretch both arms way out wide and grasp each side of the podium as though you have just captured it. Don't turn the podium into a crutch to give you support. Your audience is smart and they'll pick up on it.

### 7. Wear Just the Right Thing

Obviously, what you choose to wear and how you choose to groom yourself will create immediate impressions. If you have a great deal of confidence and experience, and if the audience already knows you, then you don't have to be quite as concerned as someone eager to make the right first impression.

Women, *short* skirts on stage distract your audience from your message and take away from the professionalism you want to project. To avoid the whole fashion issue on exactly which length is hip at the moment, I have given up and moved on to very elegant pantsuits when I am speaking. Every now and then, the occasion requires a skirt or dress, and so I opt for a professional, conservative length. That is the safest route for those who want to be taken seriously.

Now, many people are simply not interested in what's "in style." That's just fine. However, even though the business dress code is generally "conservative," it *is* important to have an overall knowledge of the basic "dos and don'ts" that are currently in style, mostly so you don't wear something downright awful. And society's standards of what "conservative" dress *is* changes at least every decade. By staying current (and it could be something as simple as choosing a tie in the hottest color of the season), you are saying to your audience that you are on top of things, you know the trends, you are informed, you can take them into the future.

There are two simple ways you can quickly and painlessly learn all you need to know about looking great on stage. First, buy any national fashion magazine in the spring and again in the fall. They are usually filled with "dos and don'ts." While most of the magazines are extreme in fashion, they do keep track of the trends in our society— something as simple as the width of a tie, perhaps.

Second, make friends with a "personal shopper" at one of the finer department stores. Just call ahead to see if you need to make an appointment, confirm that their services are free, and ask if they expect a minimum purchase. After spending some time with you, they will keep you posted

about what would look perfectly "in" for your fashion personality, and they'll notify you when those items go on
sale!

As you dress for your moment in the spotlight, make
sure there are no wrinkles in your clothes and no spots.
Men, check the color and the length of your socks. No
white socks with dark pants, for instance. And make sure
that when you cross your legs, skin doesn't show. Women,
you might want to take an extra pair of nylons *just in case.*
Everyone should check their shoes and make sure they are
buffed and look well cared for. Believe it or not, your
shoes *are* noticed.

One high-level executive at a large American company
once commented that whenever he interviews a candidate
for employment and that candidate performs well in every
category, he looks at the candidate's shoes. The shoes then
determine whether or not the person is hired. If the person has polished and shined his shoes, he gets hired, if
not, he's passed by. Why?

By making sure that your shoes are polished and
shined, you give the immediate impression that the rest of
your business or personal affairs are handled with the
same attention to detail. By the same token, if your hair or
your shirt looks unkempt or sloppy, it will send the
impression that you do sloppy work.

### 8. Pay Attention to Your Makeup and General Appearance

Because grooming of the hair and face are such personal issues, I will only say this: pay attention to what TV
news personalities are doing with hair and makeup. They
have highly paid consultants to come in and give them
"the look" that is theoretically the most credible to their
viewership. Why not borrow from them and make it work

for you? And notice that the women on TV rarely, if ever, wear *red* nail polish. It's distracting.

For further information on the latest fashion tips, you may want to look up a few of these sites on the Web:

www.dressforsuccess.com

www.fashion.net

www.womenswire.com/9to5

### 9. Be Prepared

Preparation—both in terms of research and practice, practice, practice—is absolutely essential to pulling off a "natural" presence on stage. Your adrenaline will be high when you walk on stage, so do everything you can to simulate that adrenaline before the time comes. Rehearse your presentation without mistakes, telling yourself that every time you make a mistake, you have to start over. That will give you a little simulated pressure to work with. Too often, people "wing it," thinking that ideas will come to them as they go along and that they will appear more natural by not rehearsing too much. Practicing or studying something over and over . . . and over again . . . until it is completely part of you will free you from wondering if you'll get it right. Once you're free from that worry, you can let go and genuinely communicate.

The troops who headed into battle on D-Day "practiced" for two years, doing maneuvers hundreds and thousands of times so when it came time to load up the thousands of watercraft to cross the channel, the men felt it was just another exercise. On April 27, just six weeks before the invasion, Allied troops participated in Exercise Tiger, a live-ammunition practice run that involved thirty thousand men and three hundred ships. *National Geographic* magazine recently told their unknown and top-secret story: "Gen.

Dwight D. Eisenhower, supreme commander of Operation Overload (Allied code for the invasion itself), was aboard an observers' ship on April 27, when Exercise Tiger went terribly wrong—failed air cover, late landing craft, confusion on the beachhead. Amphibious tanks, heading to shore, misaimed their guns and wounded soldiers on the beach. At least one of the tanks sank in choppy seas while its frantic crew managed to escape. . . .

"Worse was yet to come. Around 2 a.m. on April 28, nine German *Schnellboote*—fast, elusive torpedo boats—pounced on a line of eight U.S. tank-landing ships, or LSTs. They were churning down the English coast toward Slapton Sands, fully loaded with vehicles and men who were to land in the next phase of Exercise Tiger. German torpedoes struck three LSTs at the end of the line. *LST-531* capsized and sank within minutes, taking hundreds of men down with her. The torpedo that hit *LST-289* crumpled her stern, but she stayed afloat and made it to port. Gasoline aboard *LST-507* exploded and set the ship afire. . . .

"Senior officers ashore, quickly assessing the damage, ordered the five surviving LSTs to continue streaming toward Dartmouth, their destination. Capt. John Doyle, commanding officer of *LST-515*, the lead ship, disobeyed the order. He turned back to look for survivors. 'We started looking for the ones who were still alive,' Brent Wahlberg, *515* gunnery officer, remembers. 'We found 132 survivors.' Many of the dead, they noticed, were floating head down, feet up, with their life belts inflated. No one had told them that the life belts were to be worn under the armpits, not around the waists. That lesson from Exercise Tiger would be taught to invasion troops, saving countless lives" (Thomas B. Allen, "Untold Stories of D-Day," June 2002, 7–8).

Walking on stage to give a speech will never match the

drama and fear of heading into war, no matter how much someone might insist that it does. But you can prepare for it just the same. Become so entrenched in the passion of your message that you are more focused on your audience and their understanding than you are on your own fears. When that happens, not only do you relax, but your audience relaxes knowing you are perfectly comfortable and in control. Your credibility also increases, and that's when the power of persuasion happens.

### 10. Surround Yourself with Encouragers

As you prepare to become more confident in front of an audience, don't hang around people who discourage you more than encourage you. Dismiss the discouragers from your life (if they are in your workplace or family, dismiss their *words*), and replace them with those who believe in you and want to build you up.

If you are especially interested in becoming a better-than-average speaker, contact the National Speakers Association at www.nsaspeaker.org.

A good friend of mine once asked me to speak at a ladies' luncheon, but I apologetically told her I would be getting back from a horseriding trip that morning and wouldn't have time to shower and change into appropriate clothing. She begged me to come anyway, saying these ladies wouldn't care what I was wearing. I begged to differ, but decided to help her out even though I would be in my jeans and would probably smell like a horse.

Before I walked into the formal banquet room that morning, I felt incredibly self-conscious and embarrassed. Why in the world did I agree to this? I decided, however, to say nothing about my feelings, but rather pretend I was wearing the most elegant ball gown ever created. I stood straight, breathed deeply, and walked in with a huge smile on my face, Levi's, eau de horsey, and all.

I decided to visit each table and introduce myself in the hopes of making friends before I had to stand before them all. (That way I would get them on my side where they were more likely to laugh with me and less likely to be critical of me.)

Later my friend told me that her luncheon ladies had never enjoyed a speaker quite as much! She said that many of them even mentioned how surprised they were that someone in jeans and boots and a ponytail could come across so professionally and in command of the stage.

Naturally, I was very flattered. And those comments secured for me even more the importance of simple things like posture, smile, attitude, and a confident voice. In other words, stage presence.

## WHEN STAGE FRIGHT IS VERY REAL

Jerry Seinfeld once quipped, "According to most studies, people's No. 1 fear is public speaking. No. 2 is death. So to the average person, if you have to go to a funeral, you're better off in the casket than doing the eulogy."

In 1967, Barbra Streisand gave a concert in New York's Central Park despite a death threat she had received before going onstage. Once on stage, "I forgot my words in front of 135,000 people," she revealed later. "I went blank." Because of that brief experience, she had stage fright so bad that it was twenty years before one of the greatest singer/actresses of our time could make it back in front of a live audience.

Stage fright can be incredibly debilitating, and most of us have felt it at one time or another. In addition to the ten steps just described, it is beneficial to understand the

stages of how someone develops into a speaker/per-
former. When you know the process, then you are less
likely to skip some of the essential elements to becoming
comfortable on stage.

### The Three Stages of Speaker/Performer Development

**1: Experience.** There's no way around this. The more
you do it, the better you'll get. Give yourself plenty of real
experience by saying "yes" to everything, even if you're
sure you will bomb. Failure is actually the best teacher of
all in this business. No matter how much you read or study
or get others to help you, the only way to become comfortable on stage is by actually *doing* it again and again. I
like to think of it as the Pavlovian conditioning approach
to improvement—a systematic desensitization and use of
similar procedures that helps you become accustomed to
anything. Anytime you do something over and over, you
will gradually become "desensitized" to the difficulties
once associated with it.

**2: Technique.** Surprisingly, the technique involved (that
is, the dynamics, the pacing, the kinds of words to use, the
phrasing) is often picked up after you have become comfortable on stage. Why? Because if you are concentrating
too much on all the things you have to do, you will not
communicate. It is best to concentrate on delivering a message, *your* message, first. Too often, people concentrate on
technique instead of message and they appear too staged,
rehearsed, or even robotic.

Once you feel good about being in front of people,
you can involve "techniques" that fit your personality. All
speakers/performers should not be alike. And the best
ones are all different. Incorporate the techniques that feel
natural—there's no one right way to do it. For instance, I

am a fast talker, so in order to give my audience time to catch up, and to be able to think about what I'm saying, I have to make sure I slow down at times, usually when I deliver my most important points. Professional speakers also make sure they never speak in a monotone voice—there are highs and lows in their speaking tones. Some speakers almost choreograph their hand gestures. There are many "techniques" you can apply if you choose (I don't recommend applying all of them; just try one at a time). You may even want to check out a book on the subject, or go online to www.nsaspeaker.org.

**3: Passion.** When a speaker or performer can finally get past the need for more experience and has discovered the technique that brings her to the next level, that's when she can put everything aside, let go, and *really* communicate. When a speaker or performer feels a genuine passion for the message, then she can effectively connect with the audience.

If stage fright is very real for you, then you likely feel that *every* time you get up in front of people to speak or perform you are venturing around the edges of your pond, purposefully looking for an ugly frog to kiss. Right now, that doesn't sound like a fun activity to pursue. But the more you search, the more those ugly frogs won't look quite as disgusting. In fact, you'll eventually get so used to warts and slimy skin that they will look perfectly normal. Keep in mind, though, that as you gather experience, much of the time it will be just like kissing a frog that does *not* turn into a prince. But then, after time, everything will come together, you'll feel comfortable with your audience and they with you. Then it will feel just like you've found the frog prince, a toad you can really fall in love with—warts and all.

Chapter 12

# IDENTIFYING
# OTHER COMMON FEARS

There are as many different zones where a person might feel comfortable—or uncomfortable, for that matter—as there are individuals. What might be hard for me could be very easy for you. Indeed, my greatest fear might be your greatest strength.

The last chapter explored one of our most common fears: speaking in front of large or small audiences. For many of us, there is nothing more frightening than the prospect of getting up in front of an audience to perform, present, or persuade. But are there other fears or personality quirks that are just as debilitating? Does your frog have more than one wart? Certainly. This chapter will explore personality traits and common fears that make it difficult for people to move outside of their comfort zones. It's likely that you are well acquainted with one of these fears. If so, remember that the only thing really hard about moving out of your particular comfort zone is taking that first step. After the first step, your comfort zone will automatically move outward with you if you decide beforehand that no matter what, failure or success, you will learn something. When you learn, your comfort zone grows—regardless of the outcome.

## SHYNESS

People who are shy know that there is nothing more frightening than suddenly becoming the center of attention—something that is often necessary when approaching the edges of your comfort zone, where frogs and toads compete for your love.

"If you are really shy, it's a horrible problem, one that prevents you from living your life fully," says Stanford University psychologist Philip Zimbardo, who is widely acknowledged as the country's leading expert on the subject. People who are incredibly shy can even suffer physical symptoms—rapid heartbeat, trembling, sweating, hot flashes—causing them to avoid making eye contact and lose the ability to articulate a point. If you feel like you have a serious problem with shyness, you may want to check out Dr. Zimbardo's book, *Shyness: What It Is, What to Do about It* (Cambridge, Mass.: Perseus Books, 1989). You could also visit the following Web site, which is devoted to helping people overcome shyness: www.shyness.com.

If you're like me, however, and you feel shy only on occasion, consider this advice: When I am feeling especially shy (and we all do at varying times and degrees) and would rather have the attention move to someone else, I become an "interviewer." I simply ask others questions about themselves. Doing so has a variety of benefits:

- You make others feel good about themselves, which in turn helps them feel good about you.
- You no longer need to be "entertaining."

- It's difficult to be "rejected," or feel rejected, when you're just asking questions.
- You will become a better listener, which is essential to becoming a good conversationalist; and that increases your confidence in social situations.
- When you ask other people questions, they will typically return the interest by asking more about you. You may not exactly want that—if you're extremely shy—but the more others can get to know you and vice-versa, the easier it will be to stretch your comfort zone.
- When you ask questions, you don't have to talk as much!
- Everyone has something interesting to say. You could learn something.
- It's good manners to encourage others to talk.

## COMPETITION

If you have a tendency to avoid competition in general—anything from community softball games to competing for a job—it may be that you fear the consequences of committing yourself to a win or a loss. The thought of losing—or even worse, doing something foolish in the process—pushes some people so deeply into their own comfort zones that they begin to think *trying* isn't even an option.

When Baron Pierre de Coubertin organized the modern Olympics in Athens, Greece, in 1896, he did it with the purpose of using competition to promote world peace: "Peace could be the product only of a better world; a better world could be brought about only by better individuals; and better individuals could be developed only by the give and take, the buffering and battering, the stress and strain of free competition."

He viewed competition as a way of fostering friendships and building inner fortitude. Today, however, competition has an ugly side; and many people think of it as a scary thing, something that pits friends against each other, creates enemies, and destroys one's self-worth. At times, people have even called competition pointless, saying it's silly to be looking for a winner when we really should be focusing on making everybody feel good about themselves.

But competition is not so much about beating out others as it is about discovering what you're made of. It is not the outcome of competition that changes you; it is the preparation and the involvement.

Baron de Coubertin once said something that has now become well known as "An Athlete's Creed" or "The Olympic Creed": "The most important thing in the Olympic Games is not to win but to take part, just as the most important thing in life is not the triumph but the struggle. The essential thing is not to have conquered but to have fought well."

My good friend Henry Marsh came to personally understand those words when he entered the competition of his life with high hopes . . . and in the end, went home with nothing but the sting of defeat and valuable lessons learned. Henry was only the second American male runner to make four Olympic teams—he spent a remarkable thirteen consecutive years as one of the top ten 3,000-meter steeplechase runners in the world. He claimed thirteen national titles, four American records, and was ranked number one in the world for three years. But he never won an Olympic gold, silver, or even bronze medal. He said, "To me, it is the spirit of Pierre de Coubertin, of never giving up, of staying the course no matter what, that is the real spirit that drives the Olympic Games. I choose to think that my Olympic experiences helped shape my life, much for the better. I know this: by not finishing first and not realizing the fulfillment of my dreams—when everyone in the world, myself included, fully expected I would—I was able to gain a much better appreciation and understanding of the Olympic Creed spoken by Baron de Coubertin. . . . It's easy to stay the course and fight the fight when you're on top, when you're winning, but what of those times when everywhere you look you see nothing but hurdles, obstacles, roadblocks, barricades, detours and swamps? That is when you find out who you are" (as quoted on the Copernicus Gateway to Education Web site, www.edgate. com/summergames/inactive/olympic_spirit/henry_marsh. html). Legendary basketball coach John Wooden, who led the UCLA Bruins to ten national championships in twelve years, says, "Saying 'I tried, but it didn't work out' is a lot better than 'I wish I had tried.'"

What is it that scares you about competition? Are you scared of competition at work or on the court or in running the potato sack race at your child's school fieldday? Are you concerned that others might see you look foolish? Or that you might not measure up to expectations?

What do you think a world-class skier feels like as she readies herself in the gate with poles dug into the snow, waiting for the signal to begin her race? Exactly what you think it might feel like—a major case of the butterflies. What do you think a concert pianist feels as he waits in the wings for his turn in front of the judges at an international piano competition? Yes, exactly. He probably feels quite ill. Competition brings out the nerves in all of us—no one is immune.

In the November 11, 2001, issue of *Sports Illustrated,* I

read about the United State's best luge duo as they headed into the 2002 Winter Olympics: Mark Grimmette and Brian Martin. Even world-class Olympic athletes are not immune from the jitters that precede competition. Right before the 1998 Olympics, where they were the first U.S. lugers favored to win, Grimmette thought he had a stomach virus, and Martin was dealing with pain from a "knot" in his back. As soon as their run was completed and they picked up the bronze medal, they both reported no more symptoms (see Brian Cazeneuve, "Inside Olympic Sports"). I imagine the same symptoms returned before the 2002 Salt Lake City Games, where, incidentally, they picked up a silver medal.

If you can't face the possibility of failure and all the nerves that inevitably go with it, you will never make it to your own "luge runs," you will never be in the position to face success.

Confront competition by first asking, "How can I beat myself?" If that becomes your primary goal, then the rest of the "competition" is secondary. Then, befriend your competition. Let them know you respect them. This demonstrates confidence, even if you don't really feel confident. Respecting your competitors enables them to become your allies at some point.

## CHANGE

You may not be shy, and you may actually like a spirited competition. If so, those are two fears you don't need to overcome when venturing outside your comfort zone. Instead, you might be one of the millions who fear something else: change. And change almost always occurs when you want to expand the boundaries of your comfort zone. Change signifies something new and unknown.

I moved many times in my youth, and each time there were the usual anxieties about making new friends, living in a new house, and going to a new school. With each move, however, the anxieties became fewer and fewer. I got used to it . . . just like anything you do over and over again. I began to view change as synonymous with *adventure,* and that's when my whole attitude toward change, well, changed. Both *change* and *adventure* deal with the unknown: both may be good or bad, both give you no idea what to expect, both make you a stronger person. We tend to look at adventure as wildly exciting when it really is all about unexpected changes. So the next time you think of change, just replace it with the word *adventure*— that should produce a whole *change* of attitude!

When my mother and father married, it was a second marriage for them both. But that was not the daunting part. My Dad had been a widower living with his three children in Asuncion, Paraguay, and once he decided that his motherless children needed a mother, he went back to the United States to find one . . . in the two months he was able to take a leave of absence!

My mom was a single parent with one daughter when they met. Seven days later they were engaged, and twenty-nine days later they were married and off on a boat to South America . . . accompanied on their honeymoon by Mom's two-year-old daughter and Dad's three-year-old son. This was Change with a capital C. My mom had never lived in a foreign country, did not speak Spanish, barely knew her new husband, and had not even met his two oldest children. But both of them chose to view this kind of change as an adventure instead of a formula for disaster.

Two years after they set up their "Brady Bunch" home in Paraguay, I was their firstborn, and I have two more sisters who came along after me. I have grown up in a household where life is very much viewed as an adventure; opportunities should be grabbed and anything can be learned . . . given time and patience!

Change is simply another opportunity for more opportunities.

## LEARNING

Learning is a stretching process, one that can be scary and exciting all at once, especially in today's high-speed world. Our society is split into those who are techno-literate and those who are not, or rather, those who refuse to be because it is outside their comfort zone. Learning requires an attitude of humility, acknowledging that, believe it or not, you don't know everything.

Two years ago I made the decision to go back to school to get my master's degree, with the plan to take just one class a semester until all my children were in school all day long—but who's counting down? This decision meant I would have to deal with being uncomfortable about two things: (1) I would have to take the GRE, the Graduate Record Exam, and score high enough to be considered for a graduate program, and (2) I would have to accept the fact that I would most likely be called "grandma" by the other students (at thirty-eight, they would surely see me as being from an entirely different generation). That didn't sound appealing, but *learning* did.

As hard as it is to juggle a graduate class with everything else (like working on a twenty-page research paper only *after* the kids get in bed), *learning* has a way of being exciting nonetheless. And every time you experience a breakthrough, even just a small one, you have stretched that comfort zone. Confidence breeds confidence.

So get out there and learn something. Sign up for a class—showing up the first day will be difficult, but after that things get much easier. If you're too scared to publicly seek a learning experience, browse the Internet or search the shelves at the library for sites and books that will help you learn more about a favorite topic. You may become so enthused about the topic that your fears of being too old or seeming too dumb will be thwarted by your desire to find out more.

## DIFFERENCES

Interacting with people of different ethnic, cultural, religious, generational, or socio-economic backgrounds presents challenges outside comfort zones for all of us, in one way or another. It might be in communicating or in overcoming racial or religious prejudice, or simply in not knowing how to help. Relationships of all kinds are constantly moving between comfort and discomfort purely because each individual is different and constantly evolving. It takes significant effort to incorporate and accept the differences of other people within your comfort zone. But don't let your differences hold you back.

This past summer I was with my children at the local water park, where we have season passes. My four-year-old son, Jacob, came running up to me where I sat reading under a shady tree.

"Mommy! Come see! There's a girl with a leg like Go-Go Gadget [referring to the movie, *Inspector Gadget*]!"

At first I couldn't figure out what in the world he was talking about so excitedly with a big smile. I could tell, however, that whatever it was, he wanted one just like it.

He grabbed my hand and proceeded to lead me over to a group of people nearby. When he stopped and turned, suddenly shy, I knew we had arrived at our destination, but I was embarrassed to find that we were standing in other people's *"space"* and nothing appeared to be highly unusual. I glanced down to follow Jacob's gaze (he was now shyly hiding behind me) and saw a pretty little blond girl just about Jacob's age, standing close to her mother. My eyes were instantly drawn to her blue eyes, and then a glare from the sun bounced off something near the ground. I looked down to see her left leg, and I immediately understood why Jacob would think of "Inspector Gadget." Her leg from the knee down was not a typical prosthesis made to look like a real leg, but was instead made of a variety of colors of what appeared to be steel and nuts and bolts. It *was* really cool looking!

I began talking to her mother and asked if I could introduce my son, who was so fascinated with her great leg. Though he was too shy to say much, I knew he was very impressed. We sat and talked for a little bit, found out that she had been born missing that part of her leg, and was quite used to functioning well with it. After a few minutes, and with obvious questions out of the way, all we could see was a beautiful four-year-old little girl.

The most important thing I wanted Jacob to learn was that just because he might see someone different from him, and maybe feel awkward about what to say or do or ask, that is not a valid reason to stay in his comfort zone and simply stare out at them. This is true for all of us. We all need to take a first step and make a connection. Once the connection is made, more often than not you will discover similarities rather than differences—which really are just a façade that will give way to the person you find inside.

## PHYSICAL CHALLENGES

Many physical challenges, from controlling a weight problem to the inability to walk to contracting a disease you can't predict, threaten to close up your comfort zone. Our bodies can and do frustrate and disappoint us. Comfort—both as a state of mind and a state of being—seems to be a never-ending quest for many with physical challenges.

Let's take weight, for example. No one *wants* to be so heavy that it's difficult to bend over easily to pick something up off the floor or walk up one flight of stairs without collapsing. But the thought of trying to remove sixty or one hundred or even two hundred or more pounds can seem impossible, and therefore hopelessly far outside your comfort zone. When I gained that sixty pounds with my last pregnancy, I was eager to step on the scales hours after Jacob was born just to see how much I had lost— after all, he was an eight-pound baby so I should have lost at *least* that much, right?

I got on the scale and about cried. I was *sixty-one* pounds over my pre-pregnancy weight. How did that happen? I did my math right . . . and that was *not* the kind of addition I had always depended on. At that moment, I thought I would never be able to lose that weight.

Most of us have had those feelings at one time or another. Weight issues are a hot topic on TV and radio talk shows, in magazines and newspapers. It seems that there are very few people who are happy with their weight.

If losing weight is something you want to do but can't seem to talk yourself into because it means a trip outside your comfort zone, you're definitely not alone. Fortunately, moving outside your zone to shed some pounds is handled exactly the same as any other trip to the edge—you must concentrate on the *first step*. This is not a new concept, but too many of us forget that and keep looking at the seeming impossibility of the situation rather than the immediate *possibility*. No, the fat doesn't come off immediately, but your effort can happen immediately. You can do something, anything, right now. And you can do something tomorrow, and the next day, and the next. Or you can do nothing and stay the same.

I have two good friends that decided enough was enough. They made the commitment, they stuck to the plan, and between the two of them they have now lost over three hundred pounds . . . and counting. You should see their huge *smiles*. My friends look great, but more important, they *feel* great. They did something hard, they left their comfort zones, and now they are enjoying the rewards that come after a hearty struggle.

Now, what about the times when you aren't allowed to choose whether or not you step out of your comfort zone, you're just shoved out? Maybe an accident keeps you down for a month, or maybe you have lost a loved one, or maybe you no longer have use of your right hand. First, go back to those absolutes. Then take action. Instead of just psyching yourself up about adjusting to the changes, talk with the right people, get involved, contribute your time, go see your physical therapist (and actually *do* what is prescribed), and basically focus on what you can do, not what you can't.

## SAYING NO!

Some people are comfortable doing anything and trying anything. In fact, some people become *un*comfortable if they have a moment of down time to relax in a stress-free zone. They simply break down when they are not "being everything to everyone." This is particularly true for mothers.

I used to say "yes" to practically everyone and their requests because deep down I'm a people-pleaser and I like making a difference wherever possible. We all like feeling needed, don't we? But I began to resent those requests because they always seemed to take me away from family or something I really wanted to do. Yet still I plugged away because I didn't like telling people "no." I felt that saying "no" was almost like saying I wasn't *capable* of what they were asking.

Then I discovered a very easy way to step out of my "yes" comfort zone, and enter the "no" zone. I set a quota for myself on the number of nonprofessional requests I can accept per month—these can be anything from a baby-sitting exchange or PTA committee assignment to speaking for the local Chamber of Commerce. Now I am no longer the "bad guy" when I apologetically say no. I just blame it on that quota and, interestingly enough, most people quickly say they understand.

With each "no" I say (very kindly and appreciatively, of course), my comfort zone is widening. I find myself taking the time to sit down and read the paper more often, and I am rarely resentful of a request I *have* accepted.

Most of us have several different comfort zones we like to hang out in—you no doubt recognized one or more throughout this chapter. If you want to move outside, however, just start with one area for now and flirt with it a little. Don't make huge plans for a grand kiss with any frog yet—just think about it for a while. Ideas will come to you gradually, and you will instinctively know where you can start.

Chapter 13

# MUSTERING UP CONFIDENCE, REDUCING STRESS, AND GETTING STARTED!

Frogs are supremely and royally patient. They can sit quietly for as long it takes to snag their victim. Now, the idea is for you to avoid becoming the victim—swallowed up because of inaction or indecisiveness. Make the first move and take control of the waiting opportunity over there on the lily pad. Let's start with the confidence issue.

## MUSTERING UP THE CONFIDENCE TO MOVE OUTSIDE THE POND

During the five years that I thought about this book and getting it finished, people would often ask me what my latest project was, and I would tell them *this book*. As soon as I mentioned "comfort zone," I always got the same reaction. The person's head would roll back, his eyes would look upward and then down again as he'd say to me, "*I* need to read *that!*" I was surprised by the number of extremely confident people who immediately connected with the concept of being stuck in a comfort zone.

Even though we all come from different backgrounds

and circumstances, all of us tend to fear—even if it's just a little—the prospect of expanding our comfort zones. Remember, however, that the first step to expansion involves one simple decision that will take you on exciting new adventures. Tell yourself, as I have done:

*I will make decisions based on courage, not fear.*

Mustering up the confidence to first decide not to give in to fear requires that you get rid of the standard excuses for leaving your comfort zone. See if you have ever thought of one or more of these:

"I'm too old to change or try new things."
"I don't have enough time."
"I have no desire to leave my comfort zone."
"I'm too tired."
"It's not important."

If you have uttered one of those phrases on occasion, vow to never use those words again. Then consider that right now is the perfect time to let go of all the stupid, embarrassing things you have ever done in your life and just clear them off that shelf in your brain. Every time you revisit one of those times you chip away at your confidence level.

After I had already been working as a TV sports reporter for five years, something relatively insignificant happened that affected me for nearly three years.

As a sideline reporter for ESPN's college football team, I was down on the field delivering my usual live report when, in one brief moment, my mind went blank. Suddenly I felt a panic I had never felt before. I thought of the millions of people watching me, wondering why I wasn't saying anything. I envisioned my producer in the production truck going crazy. Though I recovered quickly enough that few people even noticed anything, that horrible feeling of panic remained with me. I had never before had a problem with remembering what I was going to say on camera. But because of that one instant, I knew it could happen again. Stress began creeping into my professional life, allowing my fear of what *could* happen to take control of my thoughts.

I was so scared everything could go wrong that I literally made myself sick every week before going on TV. I wanted to quit, to switch careers. The only person I told about this problem was my husband. In fact, I told him I would rather go through labor than get back on TV. He was sure I would get over it and just kept saying it would go away the more I worked. I think he instinctively knew that if he *had* made a big deal out of it, it would have become one. In the meantime, however, it felt like a real problem for me and I worried that it would affect my entire career.

Yet I knew I couldn't quit.

Every week, starting as early as Monday, I began to feel ill about the upcoming game when I would have to talk to a "live" camera. It got bad enough that I even toyed with the idea of going to see a sports psychologist, which was becoming a popular thing to do among athletes. But because I was working in the world of sports and had a number of athletes I could call for advice, I decided to do some of my own research to see how others got over their fears and dealt with the stress of playing/performing well every day.

I read about baseball players who suddenly and mysteriously forgot how to throw a baseball. Steve Sax with the L.A. Dodgers, for example, made a bad throw, started thinking about it too much, and kept making more bad throws. Finally, at the All-Star Game in 1983, in front of a national audience, he bounced a throw in front of the first baseman who was less than forty feet away from him. After that, when a player had a mental block and couldn't throw, it was dubbed the "Steve Sax disease"—although he certainly was not the only player who had experienced this dilemma. To "cure" him, the Dodgers tied a sock over Sax's eyes and made him throw balls to first base blindfolded. The thing that finally got him over this "illness" was visualizing strong, accurate throws.

Seven-time all-star Dale Murphy started out his pro career as a catcher but developed a block about the simple act of throwing the ball back to the pitcher. The cure? He was moved to the outfield where he became a five-time Golden Glove winner.

Former major league manager Chuck Tanner saw his share of this strange disease: "If you worry about failing, you will. The biggest reason behind these throwing mysteries is players trying not to make mistakes. You can't play that way. You have to play the way you did when you were a kid and not be afraid" (in Richard Demack, "Mysterious Malady," *Sports Illustrated,* 8 April 1991, 44–47).

This all made me wonder if I should go back to my original thought of changing careers—*maybe working off camera, behind the scenes would be better,* I thought. I read about basketball players who couldn't find the basket after leading the team in points. And gymnasts who could no longer stay on the beam, although they had been perfectly balanced for years.

The day before I covered a Michigan football game in 1992 as part of my Big Ten football assignment, I chatted with Wolverine quarterback Elvis Grbac for a while and asked him how he got over his fears—like performing poorly or getting sacked. He told me about a book he carried around with him and was studying diligently: *You Can't Afford the Luxury of a Negative Thought* (Life 101 Series, Peter McWilliams, Los Angeles: Prelude Press, 1997). He said that it really was helping him to focus on his talents instead of allowing doubts to creep in and wreak havoc. So I went right over to the Michigan bookstore and bought a copy. The next day, Elvis took quite a beating by the defense in the first half and was sacked several times. But he kept going back in, seemingly unfazed. I just happened to have that book in my backpack, so I pulled it out and asked the producer to let me talk about Elvis. When the camera's red light went on, I felt strangely comfortable talking about how Elvis was reading this book that apparently was helping him to see past all those nasty defensive linemen and to concentrate on his game. He won the game for them . . . and I started reading the book.

I also remembered the story of my friend, Elaine Zayak, whom I met in 1984 when we had a joint appearance for a sponsor. In 1982 Elaine entered the U.S. Figure Skating Championships as the reigning national champion, but in the space of four minutes she fell three times. One month later at the World Championships, Elaine was still reliving those humiliating falls, and just hours before she was scheduled to skate she was hysterical. She told her coaches she would not go on. She was engulfed with fear as she remembered what had happened in Indianapolis.

Elaine explained to her coaches that she had gone for years and had never missed a landing in competition, and now that she knew she could, she just couldn't go through with it. So she told her coaches that if they loved her, they wouldn't make her skate. They replied that they loved her, but that she needed to try it one more time. Desperately hoping to find a way to calm her down, her coaches brought an old and trusted friend to her room who sat her down and put things in perspective for her. He told Elaine that what she was feeling was nerves, not fear. He explained the difference in this way: when you go to a fancy restaurant and you order a very expensive meal and you have $100 in your pocket, you're nervous. You're not fearful. You're *fearful* when you go the restaurant and you have no money in your pocket and you order a big dinner. You don't have the capability of paying anything. He said to Elaine, "You have the $100—you have the capability. Tonight you will do your best. It may not be enough, but you will not embarrass yourself. You have the ability."

She dried her tears, got ready for the competition, and that night, Elaine Zayak became champion of the world!

I could relate to the anxiety she had felt at that moment, and I knew that somehow, I had to focus on that "$100 in my pocket" instead of those nerves. I wanted to rid myself of the "paralysis of analysis"—that circumstance in which a person makes one mistake or notices one flaw in a performance and then begins to analyze that mistake until he or she becomes paralyzed with fear and is unable to have the confidence needed to perform well. I decided to analyze my case of nerves instead of my mistakes.

Because I would typically come down with a stomachache about five days before I had a "live" report, I wondered if it would be possible to cut that time down (I knew it wasn't realistic for me to expect a complete disappearance of nerves right away) in order to help myself get more sleep and thus feel better prepared. Realizing that *more* nerves did not mean *better* nerves, I convinced myself that I really didn't need to be sick for five days, just a few hours would do. The first time I tried it, it worked. I knew I could relax because I had built in the time to be nervous *later*. So instead of being nervous for five days, I was nervous just the Saturday *morning* before the game. I gave myself the realistic permission of cutting down the sick time.

The next game, I cut down my allowable "nervous" time even more, and again it worked. I was beginning to feel more in control of myself, and not quite so mentally exhausted. By the end of the season, I was down to what I called my "five-minute nervous window"—those five minutes right before the red light goes on and the producer starts counting down in my ear. It was okay for me to be nervous for those five minutes because, in a way, that told me I was completely alert and focused and not distracted by other things.

To this day I still "program" those five minutes almost as a way of telling myself that I can use them if I want to. But after eighteen years of working in television it is now a wonderful and satisfactory feeling to rarely draw from that bank of nervous "butterflies."

## OVERCOMING SETBACKS THAT AFFECT CONFIDENCE

In 1993, the athlete I had come to know and like through the interviews I did with her was stabbed in the back as she rested between games at a competition in Hamburg, Germany. Monica Seles, one of the most powerful tennis players on the women's tour at that time, was not only badly injured physically, but mentally as well. She was stripped of her confidence, and for two years she struggled to regain her old self, trying to push thoughts away of that dark day when a deranged Steffi Graf fan tried to kill her.

While there were many in the sports world who

thought we would never see her back on the court, I knew her well enough to know that she was a classic champion. She has the mind of a champion and will not willingly allow herself to be defeated. I knew she would fight back. She would regain control over her thoughts and fears.

At the 1995 Canadian Open, Monica Seles made a stunning comeback, winning the Open 6–0, 6–1. Later she described her mental challenges. "I still backtrack. To this day, to this afternoon, there are times when your mind starts going the other way, and you can't do that. You have to get your mind to go the right way and not have those bad thoughts. I have to tell myself, 'Focus, Monica, focus.'"

## REDUCING STRESS

It's quite difficult to feel confident about making changes in your life, or adapting to change, when you feel overrun by stress. Being "stressed out" is not an enjoyable condition. When you're stressed, you have no desire to accomplish anything, let alone *start* anything—all you want is for someone to come take over your life for a few hours (or even days and maybe weeks!), put it all in order, take care of the hard things, and then hand it back to you trouble-free.

A good friend of mine likes to say, "I was born to accomplish many things. But I am getting so far behind that I'll *never* be able to die!" One revealing cartoon I recently saw shows a man plopped in front of the TV with glazed, fixed eyes. "Don't turn on the 10 o'clock news," he says to his wife. "I'm still trying to cope with the 6 o'clock news."

If you can relate to the sentiments expressed in that cartoon, it's likely that you know a little about the negative impacts of stress. For many, stress is precisely why they don't even want to think about taking a step outside of their comfort zones—there are too many demands already inside that are consuming their time and brainpower. But can that be changed?

The American Academy of Family Physicians reports that 66 percent of all office visits to family doctors are due to stress-related syndromes. Some medical authorities believe that up to 90 percent of all illnesses are stress-related. Stress is also linked to six of the leading causes of death in the United States, which include heart disease, cancer, lung ailments, accidental injuries, cirrhosis of the liver, and anxiety (see Kevin Lamb, "Stress Control: Finding a Level That Helps Rather than Harms," *The Washington Times,* 2 February 2001, D4).

During my Miss America year, I participated in a Pro-Am golf tournament. My foursome included Johnny Miller, former President Gerald Ford, and Bob Hope. Because I was no standout golfer, I wasn't intimidated in the slightest. What would be the point? I decided to thoroughly enjoy this singular experience.

When I wasn't off in the rough looking for my ball, I took turns riding with my golfing buddies. As I rode with Bob Hope in his air-conditioned golf cart, I asked him about his secret to youth (he was about eighty years old and seemed like he was having the time of his life). He said with a smile, "I learned a lesson from my friend Ronald Reagan years ago. Get a massage at least every other day. That's all it takes."

Wow, doesn't that sound great? Massages and golf. There is something profound about the simplicity of his formula. In reality, it's a great formula, I have to admit. But for those of us who have neither the time nor the financial resources to commit to a life of massages and golf (at least every other day anyway!), are there alternatives?

I have a friend who takes his instructional Yoga DVDs with him on the road to help cut down the stress that constant work and travel inevitably creates. Once he gets to his hotel room, he sets up his laptop and pops in the DVD. When I was traveling full time with ESPN, the first thing I would do after a long day when I was too tired to actually exercise—meaning, break a sweat—is stretch out. Rather than just lying there staring mindlessly at the TV until I fell asleep, stretching the muscles in my legs, back, neck, and arms helped ease my tension. It's amazing how much tension you feel just from sitting all day in planes or cars. I didn't know about yoga back then, but I guess that's why I like it so much now—it is a stress-reducing, *relaxing* exercise (if you can call any exercise *relaxing*, it's yoga!). You should try it sometime!

Exercise is the single best attack on stress there is . . . period. When you start exercising, pick something you like to do because whatever it is you like, that is what you will do. And change it around, or "cross-train." Do a different kind of exercise every day so you don't let your body, or your mind, get in a rut. I made up my own "lunge" routine (that's when you "lunge" or step forward with one foot onto a short platform and then push off, and switch legs) that I do while watching a favorite TV show. Maybe you like to run or walk. Go for a hike, or ride a bike. Maybe join a fitness club (where they have yoga classes . . . hint, hint). My husband bought me a Stairmaster (a good one that doesn't break down) for Christmas one year and I actually prefer using that over going to the gym because (a) I don't have to drive to the club, and (b) I get to watch my own TV program or a video I've wanted to see while I'm exercising. But if you're close to a gym, that's a fun way to choose many different forms of exercise. By all means, make exercise *fun*.

What if just the thought of exercise fills you to your eyeballs with stress? That's okay. Just put on some exercise clothes every day and then do whatever you would like to do. Someday the urge will hit you to actually try out the sneakers, and before you know it, you'll be an exercise zealot.

In addition to exercise, what else can you do to push stress away from blocking the runway on which you would like to take off? Here are a few stress relievers to consider:

1. Go outside and, if there's little or no pollution, take a deep breath.

2. Put on sweats—get comfortable.

3. Drink a cup of Stephen's Gourmet Hot Cocoa— Irish Crème, Mint Truffle, or fat-free Milk Chocolate are my favorites.

4. Sleep in one day—or sleep ten hours, whichever comes first.

5. If you have children, lock yourself in your room for about ten minutes . . . maybe read or take a bath.

6. Make a plan for the day, and make your children make a plan (that way you don't have to nag them—the stress is on *them*).

7. Expect for things to go wrong. When they don't, you'll be pleasantly surprised. If I come home expecting my children to have the house straightened and looking great, I will be stressed the moment I set foot in the door. (Don't, however, let your children know your expectation level is low—you *want* them to think that you expect a

clean house.) Low expectations on *your* part help keep down the stress that comes from unmet expectations.

8. Watch a good movie. Eat popcorn. With no butter.

9. Sit for a minute. Maybe even lay down for five.

10. Always keep a good book in the car with you for those times you have to wait, (traffic jams, kids at lessons, doctors' offices, and so on). Then you'll be caught up in the story instead of watching the clock and impatiently tapping your foot.

11. Think of all the activities you are committed to in a week . . . and delete one.

12. Do what you can in a given day; don't worry about what you can't do.

13. Strive for your best, not perfection.

14. Don't procrastinate.

15. Let me repeat number 14: Don't procrastinate. So much stress is avoided when projects are done well in advance.

16. Give away junk and stop buying useless and unnecessary items. Shopping might reduce stress temporarily but the results of shopping add up to stress later on in the form of bills and more *stuff* to keep organized.

17. Forget about the negative things that people do or say to you.

18. Think of a compliment to pay someone and then tell them. If they're any good at accepting compliments, you should get an immediate and healthy dose of appreciation right back at you. Appreciation, the knowledge that someone else is grateful to you, is amazingly effective.

19. Give yourself plenty of time to get where you're going, and to do what you're doing. Then if you're early, you have your book with you!

20. Keep a water bottle in the car for yourself, and if applicable, the tired, thirsty children in the back.

21. Cut down or eliminate foods that are high in fat, sugar, or salt. Eat less, but don't "diet."

22. Say no. But say yes to the children a little more often.

23. Call a good friend who makes you laugh.

24. Do something for someone else. Make a difference.

25. Pray.

## USING CONFIDENCE TO COMBAT STRESS AND ANXIETY

Our society is quite familiar with the concepts of "visualizing" and thinking "positive thoughts." It's nothing new. Today, high-level athletes use it as part of their *routine*. It's a normal part of their plan for success and works well to reduce stress and anxiety. So, shouldn't you try to apply the same principles in your stressful life and see if they help you to transition from the waters of your own comfort zone to the areas outside, where your goals and dreams await?

As I have worked through the ups and downs of confidence, there have been many things I have learned along the way that have helped me to *appear* confident even if I don't feel it. Knowing the tricks that give the *illusion* of confidence is often all you need to get going:

**1. Give a firm handshake with solid eye contact.** Never, ever, offer a weak handshake. That's the first thing that will give the impression that you lack confidence. But if you deliver a good, strong handshake, together with direct eye contact (don't let your eyes wander), the other person will immediately assume you've got confidence.

**2. Maintain good posture.**

**3. Smile!** Only people who are scared to death don't smile.

**4. Get fit.** There it is again. (You're probably wondering by now if there's any problem that can't be solved by exercise.) Anyone who gets into a consistent fitness routine and sticks with it becomes a more confident person. When you have more energy and generally feel better about yourself, it spills over into other areas where confidence is needed. Exercise really is a cure-all for so many of today's maladies.

**5. Speak up.** You don't need to speak loudly; just strongly, so people can hear you well. A barely audible voice does not project confidence.

**6. Listen more.** You don't have to say something all the time. Constant chatter is a sure sign of nervousness.

**7. Be willing to admit you're wrong or that you don't know something.** Only people with a lot of confidence can do that. And don't give a slew of excuses in doing so. That just makes you look weak. When people can admit they're wrong and they're taking steps to change their errors, that projects strength not weakness. It says you don't have to hide behind excuses, and it also sends the message that you are confident in your ability to get to the bottom of the mistake and fix it if possible. And when you say that you don't know (when you really don't know) but that you will find out, it shows a confidence in your resourcefulness and intelligence.

**8. Ask questions.** Ask people about themselves and about what they do. If you're always interested in learning, and not so intent on proving how smart you are, people will assume you're smart, and confidently so. And they'll like you too.

**9. Give credit to others when it's due.** Only those who

doubt their own abilities are afraid to talk up the abilities of others. And besides, you will win allies along the way.

**10. Be firm, with honorable standards**. Only people who are unsure, confused, and low on self-esteem have no kind of standards, or "absolutes." Be known as one who is quietly secure about her foundation of confidence.

**11. Be willing to try the hard things.** Confident people are fully aware of the risk of failure, and sometimes even fear it greatly, but take on the challenge anyway.

**12. Speak positively.** Regardless of what's going on inside of you that may not make you feel terribly positive, fake it. The more you sound positive, the more everyone around you will think you are positive—and that spells confidence.

## GETTING STARTED

Okay, you've defined your dreams, built up your confidence, reduced some of the stress in your life, and now you're ready for a real commitment. So let's go get that dream. Where do you start?

### Research

Before taking any steps in any direction—whether it's weight loss or starting a business—research anything and everything about that subject. Interview people who have done it, search the Web, read books. The more you know about it, the less intimidating it is, and thus, the more comfortable you are with the idea of embracing it.

### Interview Those Who Have Done What You Would Like to Do

Find out how others did it. Pick someone you admire in the area you would like to be better in, and then ask them to chat with you about it. Successful people love to explain "how they did it." Not only will you get great ideas but you will also feel empowered just by talking to those who have gone before you. And truly successful people know how to be encouraging. Their courage will rub off on you.

### Find a Mentor

Mentors can speed up the learning curve and help you avoid many of the mistakes they made. I have had a mentor in absolutely every endeavor I have pursued and it has made all the difference. So how do you find one? If no one stands out right away, do interviews as part of your research. Make sure each person you interview has a solid reputation. After looking over the information you pick up, zero in on the person you learned the most from then contact the person again. Let him or her know how much they influenced you, and ask if he or she could mentor you or just help you out. Usually the person will be flattered.

Another way to learn from the best is by reading biographies and taking notes. Have a notebook and pencil with you the entire time and jot down ideas as you read about that person. It is always encouraging to read about how great people overcame their insecurities—you will be able to relate, and thus make it easier to envision yourself being just as successful.

### Create a Detailed Plan

No matter what the venture may be, *anything* that takes you out of your comfort zone will be that much easier when a plan is laid out. Just as anyone who is starting a business must first write up a business plan, so it is with anything you really want to do that might be a little (or a lot) difficult.

Let's say you want to reconcile with a family member

you haven't spoken to for twenty years. You could just call up the person on the phone. But because you may worry about a number of things, such as being rejected, a plan will help move things along by leaving fear out of the picture. First, write up a list of pros and cons for the reconciliation. For the sake of this example, let's say the "pros" win. Next, write up all the possible ways to contact this family member and all the possible outcomes. List them in order of preference so if one doesn't work you can go on to the next. Write down the worst thing that can happen. If you can survive with what the worst could possibly be, then you can begin your plan by hoping for the best but being prepared for the worst.

Without a plan, people keep thinking about everything that can go wrong. This makes us feel disorganized in a way. With a plan, you can know what the worst is and thus deal with it before it ever becomes a reality.

Let your plan carry all the stress for you so you don't have to wonder what will happen. You will already know all the options.

### Can You Aim Higher?

After making a plan, check to see if you could aim a little higher. If your plan is to approach several small businesses to find funding for a talented group of young singers, could you take your proposal to one large business and offer an exclusive sponsorship? Think bigger; you can always scale it down later. Big things happen when you think big.

When you do something *more difficult* than you had originally planned, it will make the first plan seem easy. When I learned to ski at age twenty-one, I felt tremendously awkward at first. That first season, I fell often and I fell hard. As I struggled to feel comfortable hurling myself down a mountain, unsure if there would be a good ending at the bottom, an old friend from high school volunteered to go with me and give me some pointers.

Scott took me to Solitude, a resort I hadn't skied yet even though it was only about a half hour away. As I looked at the map of the resort I pointed to all the runs with green circles (it was highly recommended that beginners stick to those runs). But Scott said no. He had a better idea. He said we were going to the other side of the mountain. Since I had seen a movie by the same name, I immediately got a little nervous about where we were going, but hey, he was my friend. He'd take care of me, right?

As we rode up on the lift, I began to notice that there were no smooth runs underneath. It was nothing but *mountains* of moguls, some of them five or six feet deep! We got off, and I looked around for the easy way down, but had no such luck. The only way down was by facing the carved-out giants.

I have to admit, in my frustration during the next two hours that it took to maneuver down one single run of moguls, I got really mad at Scott. He laughed. But then an amazing thing happened. I finally reached the groomed runs, and suddenly it was incredibly easy to ski on smooth-packed powder! In one afternoon, I went from beginner to intermediate because Scott literally pushed me out of my comfort zone. From then on I bypassed the green circles, looked for the intermediate blue squares, and on occasion, even dared to take on a black diamond.

I decided I would remain Scott's friend.

One summer my husband, Bob, and I took our mountain bikes up the canyon where I anticipated we would have a good workout on a smooth path. But he and my friend Scott are a lot alike. Bob saw a tiny opening in the forest leading away from the road and said, "This way! Follow me!" Since the path was only three inches wide and flanked by trees everywhere, with tree roots sticking up at least two feet out of the ground and poison ivy covering the forest floor, I opted to get off and walk the bike through. Bob turned around, saw me taking the wimpy way out, and challenged me to be a man . . . or something like that. Since I wanted to impress him with my willingness to try and keep up (and I didn't want him to come back and make me go in tight circles), I got on and thought of all those moguls I had once faced (face down mostly).

Three things happened. One, I actually kept up with Bob most of the time. Two, I felt proud of myself. And three, just as I had learned from the skiing experience, the things that had made me nervous before—like simple graveled roads or dirt roads with a few rocks—now looked easy.

I recently came across an academic treatise in which a professor took other teachers to task for not insisting that students leave their comfort zones more often. Author Marshall Gregory wrote:

"Too often both students and teachers alike fail to operate from a belief that the best version of a student's ethos as a student is taking that big risk of going outside of the self, accepting grades lower than A's while trying to earn them, being humble enough to concede that *the standards for success exist outside of the comfort zone*, and finally, believing that this kind of humility is appropriate for getting an education.

"Education is too limited, by trying to fit notions of comfort as if discomfort meant that something is going wrong. I know that when I encounter criticisms or compelling versions of ideas I disagree with I feel uncomfortable, but I also know that *in that discomfort lie the seeds of my own learning.* Why do we teachers so often teach as if our students were too frail to endure this kind of discomfort—and to then enjoy the growth that may follow from it? Or is it that we think them insufficiently deserving of the challenge?" ("Initiation Rights: Giving First Year Students What They Deserve," *College Teaching,* 22 March 1997, 63; emphasis added).

After reading this article, I was surprised to find this very attitude with my daughter's teacher at the local elementary school. As my daughter and I joined this teacher for a conference, we reviewed my daughter's past performance. In all the categories, she had scored between 94 and 100 percent. The teacher congratulated her fine performance and then asked her, "Now what would you like your goal to be in the coming quarter?" I was proud to hear my daughter say with a smile, "100 percent." Expecting to hear her teacher say something like, "Well, good for you. That's great to aim high," she said instead, "Are you sure?"

My daughter turned to me, looking a little confused, and I looked at the teacher. Surprised by her response, I admit I was speechless. The teacher continued, "It's nearly impossible to get a 100 percent in everything. Are you sure you still want to go for that?" Curious to see what my daughter would say, I waited. A little more shyly this time, she said, "Yes." I patted her back, and still in shock over the teacher's hesitancy to push good students to do even better, I explained, "In our family we always try to shoot for the stars—we might miss them but we're better for it."

I was very proud of my daughter that day. And you

know, I don't really care that she hits 100 percent, because I know she's doing something more important. She's *shooting* for 100 percent.

When we challenge ourselves by doing the hard things and aiming high, then at least *something* will be accomplished, and it usually won't be as difficult as we anticipated.

### Do It More

A man recently asked me how he could become more comfortable with surfing since that was apparently something outside of his comfort zone. That's quite simple, really. Do it more.

Naturally, he liked that answer. Excelling at the piano, for instance, is a long, hard process. But the more I practiced, the better I got and consequently, the more I liked it. I began playing when I was seven years old and didn't like it until I was about fourteen. So when my children complain, I'm not concerned. That's normal. They're uncomfortable with having to learn hard things. They don't like that four-letter word . . . *work*. But that's fine. I know that the more they work, the easier the task will become, and then they'll be comfortable. And that's when they'll like it.

The first move toward your goal is typically one filled with anxiety and adrenaline. The most prevalent thought swirling around in that central command post in your head is probably, *What if I fail?* If it is, tell yourself, *so what?* That's better than always wondering *what if?* Then pick one thing to reduce your stress—it will take your mind off the ugly frog you're about to kiss. Finally, go ahead and take that first step toward one of the frogs you have identified as a potential prince. How can you tell which ones are the sure thing? You can't . . . but that's what makes this whole trip outside your comfort zone such an adventure! The more frog kissing you do, the more of an expert you will become until you *will* be able to identify your perfect match.

Good luck!

There's a World of
Possibility Hiding Behind
the Face of an Ugly Frog!

In Conclusion

# FIVE RULES
# TO REMEMBER

The swampy shoreline of a pond truly does differ from the waters deep within it. But the edges of your comfort zone—even those areas outside of it—aren't really that different from the areas within your zone. And once you have ventured outside your comfort zone, you're likely to discover that comfort is attainable on the outside as well. You'll also discover that the people who encouraged you inside your zone will still be there when you move outside.

It's funny how the simple, imaginary line you draw around yourself—and your "zone"—defines in your mind what you can or cannot do. Remember Robert Schuller's question: "What would you do if you knew you couldn't fail?" That's a provocative question because it forces us to confront the fact that there *are* boundaries in much of our thinking and in our actions. Some of those boundaries are good because they come in the form of rules for social and moral conduct. Other boundaries, however, act like high, barbed wire fences that keep us from discovering our true potential.

The goal of this book was to help you tear down those boundaries and discover who you are and how well you can survive outside of your comfort zone, where growth, success, happiness, and even fun are found. So, before you quit reading and begin mulling over all the frogs that you could kiss, follow the advice in the following five pointers and return to these pages often for a quick and motivational refresher course.

## 1. FACTOR IN THE PAST AND MOVE ON, QUICKLY

Everyone has some kind of a comfort zone and a number of things that lie outside that zone—maybe living alone makes you uneasy, or maybe you're afraid of the word *commitment,* or maybe you cringe at the thought of being in the spotlight. To avoid these things, you have set limits. And although your own limits depend on a number of factors, I imagine that if you think about it a little, you'll discover that your limits are based on one thing: how you have chosen to react to your *past.* Past failures, past experiences, and past relationships add up to preconceived ideas about what you *think* will happen if you do leave your comfort zone . . . if you do set out to explore and maybe even take the chance to kiss a frog or two.

Everyone has experienced some of the good and some of the bad. The difference between those who come out on top and those who don't manage to muddle through is found in their reaction to the event.

In the past, you may have chosen to react with anger, revenge, or escape. But the good thing today is that you can decide right now to react *differently* in the future. You can choose to do what I've learned to do when faced with failure and the reminders of my past: throw out the past—including the accompanying memories—altogether and *move on*. Box it up, clear it out, and make the move. Then you'll find you have storage space for new adventures—that includes new failings *and* new successes.

## 2. ANSWER THE CALL TO ACTION

Everyone wants to make life better—for themselves and their families. We want to do better than before and be better people than we were the day before. We all *want* to achieve. The trouble comes when someone yells "action" and it's time to turn wishful thinking into reality. What often happens then? Well, a great many of us peek through the curtains at the scary world outside, start to think our chances don't look so good, and head back to the La-Z-Boy recliner where we can relax in isolation. "Whew! Just narrowly missed acting on the urge to try something that might make me look stupid in the end . . . like a failure."

Have you ever wanted to apply for a different job, and just as you were about to face the personnel director for an interview, felt your heart preparing to perform a rap number? "I can't do this! They won't want me! He will see me shaking . . . I should just leave." Some people actually do leave, and others take the chance.

John Wooden, former head basketball coach at UCLA, said: "No team has ever played a perfect game. It's impossible. But *striving* for perfection is not. You have the power to do that. And when you do, you become a winner regardless of the score."

## 3. EXERCISE COURAGE—EVEN IF IT'S THE SIZE OF A MUSTARD SEED

In the New Testament, Jesus tells his disciples: "Verily I say unto you, If ye have faith as a grain of mustard seed, ye shall say unto this mountain, Remove hence to yonder place; and it shall remove; and nothing shall be impossible unto you" (Matthew 17:20).

Do you know how big a mustard seed is? When my husband and I were in Israel some years ago, we came across a mustard plant on one of our outings. I reached up, wanting to grab a few seeds to take home as visual aids. I expected something small to fall into my hands but was taken back by what I got. I had retrieved a handful of leaves and what I thought were seeds. To my surprise, what I actually had in my hands were the pods that contain the seeds. One of the pods had broken and the actual seeds, hundreds of them, had fallen out. Each seed was literally the size of the period at the end of this sentence. I put them all in a baggie and stowed them in my purse. My friends back home were amazed to find that faith the size of a barely discernible seed could move mountains.

Courage falls in the same category as faith. We just need enough to help us get through the door. The difference between those who venture one small step outside their comfort zone and those who zealously guard their zone from within is courage the size of a mustard seed.

## 4. STRETCH YOUR PARAMETERS

It's safe to assume that success *is* something you want in your life. I bet that somewhere in the back of your mind, you realize that taking chances is akin to the trapeze artist swaying from the rafters—one swing and he might grab hold of the facing bar and land on the opposite platform. Or, one swing and he might fall into the net below. It may be frightening to be the trapeze artist, but if you don't even try to swing, you become nothing more than a fascinated member of the audience. To help you get up on that platform, sweaty palms and all, I suggest that you learn to recognize your comfort zone and then do something every day that stretches those parameters.

For example, if speaking in front of groups is your greatest fear, join the community council, which, by itself, doesn't usually involve public speaking. Then nominate yourself to co-chair a committee. You'll *have* to give a simple public speech to do this. What's next is the really scary part: people vote. You might lose, like I did not too long ago. Most of us do. So? Be a gracious loser, participate in the committee, and the next time, put your name up for consideration again. And if you lose again? Don't stop trying. I promise it gets easier. I've done it a thousand times.

## 5. REMEMBER, WHEN THE POND ISN'T GROWING, IT'S SHRINKING

And now, the million-dollar question: why leave your comfort zone? It's simple. If you are not growing and improving, then you are shrinking and becoming less and less sure and able. It's a subtle thing . . . so subtle that you wouldn't notice it for years maybe. But there is no such thing as a stagnant, *living* thing. You are either growing or shrinking. So ask yourself, which sounds more appealing? If that doesn't make you start moving, consider this thought from American opera composer Gian Caorl Menotti: "Hell begins on the day when God grants us a clear vision of all that we might have achieved, of all the gifts which we have wasted, of all that we might have done which we did not do."

Rose Kennedy, who went through more than her share of difficulties, said: "Believe in yourself, trust in God, then let go and enjoy the adventure!"

Why do I keep leaving my comfort zone? All I have to do is think back to the time as a college sophomore when I chose to leave my comfort zone to audition for the Young Ambassadors. When I think of all the things that happened subsequently—amazing opportunities that I had never even dreamed of—I'm fearful to *not* step out of my comfort zone, fearful that I might miss out on another adventure.

What if?

# INDEX